When Do I Clap? ©

A Slightly Irreverent Guide to Classical Music
and
Concert Hall Conduct

by

Valerie Cruice

"The applause of a single human being is of great consequence."

Samuel Johnson
from *Life of Johnson* by James Boswell
July 21, 1763

TWO BYTES PUBLISHING, LT(
• 1997 •

D1364828

Copyright © 1997 by Valerie Cruice
First Printing September 1997

Cover Art by Thomas Fowler

Produced and Published by:
Two Bytes Publishing, Ltd.
P.O. Box 1043
83 Old Kingshighway South
Darien, Connecticut 06820-5407

ISBN: 1-881907-13-9 *(soft cover edition)*

*Printed in
the United States of America*

Dedication

To My Husband, Jay,
and our children~
Kinsey, Seth and Halley

Table of Contents

Illustrations and Charts

Foreword

If you have already gotten to the point where you have picked up a copy of this book, chances are you want to know more about Classical music. You may have noticed that so many guides seem to be written for connoisseurs or presuppose a specific knowledge. But if you need something to take you through the ABCs of it – this volume will do just that. For here, in a clear, concise and witty way, you will be exposed to the basics, and Classical music will become that much more accessible to you.

Something I have noticed over the years, people love listening to music. Surely, it is one of the most powerful and profound symbols that exists. Music exalts the spirit, makes us feel happy, sad, excited, mellow. It also connects us to our history and our heritage. Since the beginning of civilization, when man first beat out a rhythm on a stick, or sang a song of love, or wept over a fallen comrade, music has made its claim on the human soul. This natural, spontaneous expression that has been used to celebrate festive and cherished occasions or to express even the most ordinary moments, has had the extraordinary power to induce moods as well as reflect how we feel.

What is music exactly? I often say that music is part of nature. It is sound – organized sound – and reflects nature's harmonies, tonalities, rhythms, mathematics, pitch, intensity, structure – *magic*! Over time, music has developed into an art form, a natural, often spontaneous, expression of personal feeling. But music also reflects our history and culture, with each generation adding to our musical inheritance.

The question arises: If one habitually listens to rock or country or popular tunes, can one take to Classical music? Of course! All musical forms can be enjoyed and on any level. The difference is that Classical music is "classic" – it stands up to the test of time, has staying power, depth, richness and complexity. It is not so trendy that you tire of it. But the good news is that you do not have to have a huge amount of knowlege to love great music. Just because music critics know more than you, does not mean they derive more joy than you do. Even having said that, I do think a deeper understanding of music will help heighten your experience and help you to appreciate and love it more.

Some say you cannot learn music from a book, you have to listen to it. Well, yes and no. Certainly, there seems to be a human need to clarify it, talk about it and read about it. So, read on, listen well, then listen and listen, and listen some more.

Peter Oundjian
Artistic Director
Center for Music and the Arts
Caramoor
Katonah, NY.

Acknowledgments

I will never forget the day when Irwin Shainman, the very distinguished professor of music at Williams College and department chairman, began "The Opera" class by flinging open the door and with his arm over his brow, hacked his way in *falsetto* across the front of the room and metamorphosed into that coughing courtesan, Violetta.

Up to that point - all my life - I had been very serious about and reverent toward *Classical Music*. While I found humor in everything else, music was untouchable as far as being funny. But not now, not any more, not after Verdi this way! Of course, we did the serious stuff, but now it took on a whole new dimension (or dementia?). I was learning while laughing, chuckling, guffawing and simply smiling, so why couldn't others?

An important figure in my development as a journalist and writer was a professor of Creative Advertising at the Colgate Darden School of Business, University of Virginia. Everard Meade had been an ace copywriter and ad man on Madison Avenue. What I learned from him was how to distill a great deal of data to its essence. The man taught me how to write a great one-liner – even if it was about cat food. Even more fun was applying this skill to music (a formidable challenge) and selling it to a reluctant or intimidated buyer.

My research took me to many concert halls, music sheds, churches, libraries, schools and private living rooms. I did not know at the time that this book would come of it, as I labored writing music reviews for local newspapers. On numerous occasions, I found audiences to be of more distraction than the orchestra, giving rise to the notion that most concert-goers do not have a clue about music, but they should be praised for having made the effort to attend the concert.

This book is for that wonderfully endearing audience which needs a bit of gentle, humorous guidance. And for those who are in the know, I've tried to throw you a few musical curve-balls throughout the movements – just to make sure you are *listening*.

I am so grateful to Elizabeth Clark of Two Bytes Publishing, Ltd., who saw the potential of this project and laughed hysterically at Chapter 5. Thank yous also go to Walt and Gaffney, and Dr. Marvin Paymer, my musical conscience.

My co-workers at the *New York Times*, Connecticut Weekly section, especially Richard Madden and Suzanne Donner – making me better, keeping me honest and allowing me to take risks.

I thank my husband, Jay, who endured cold dinners, rejection letters and my paranoia about his own clapping. My children, Kinsey, Seth and Halley, who gave me insights into the special power of music over the sandbox set – maybe now we have time to get to a concert (now that you are nearly teenagers).

And Janina, who gently encouraged me.

All my friends, but especially Amy, Carol, Eileen and Gwynne who read chapters, kept me going and have been there during the dark moments.

Joan Panetti, of the Yale School of Music, for making time for me to talk about anything but music and for being such an extraordinary role model.

Pozzi Escot, professor of music at Wheaton College, who taught me the scientific and mathematical aspects of music and how music is an integral part of life, not an isolated indulgence.

Tom Fowler, a man of quiet genius who designed this book's cover.

My sister, Jean, who is always full of spunky encouragement.

But most of all I thank my mother and father for giving me the gift of music – not to mention the thousands of piano lessons. Have I earned the Steinway, yet?

Prelude

What is Classical Music, Anyway?

"Good music isn't nearly so bad as it sounds."

Harry Zelzer
Chicago Impresario

Prelude

What Is Classical Music Anyway?

Classical music is all around us. It finds its way into our lives, almost without our knowing it – cutting through socio-economic boundaries, appealing to all intellectual capacities, permeating everyday existence through television and radio commercials, cartoons, movies and even through the computer. You have heard the phrase, "wake up and smell the coffee"; however, in this case, it is "tune in and savor the music".

By opening your ears and your mind, you will discover that Classical music can enrich the way you think, feel and express yourself. What do you hear when you listen to Classical music?

Try a test – take a piece of paper, tear it in half, on one half write down all the good things you think or feel about Classical music and on the other half write down all the bad things. Now compare the two lists! The *good* adjectives might be "awesome", "soothing", "thrilling", "other-worldly", "dignified" or "powerful". The *bad* adjectives might include descriptions such as "highbrow", "intimidating", "formal", "snobbish" or "square". Those items on your "bad" list are what Classical music is usually accused of, but these thoughts come only out of fear and lack of exposure. Exceptions may be Peter Schickele's wonderful "discovery" of P.D.Q. Bach or Victor Borge with his abundance of humor.

In reading about the composers described later in this book, whose creative output is, in fact, the source of all this anxiety, you will discover that they, indeed, were fallible human beings (as well as musicians, singers and conductors, for that matter).

If you already enjoy Classical music, *When Do I Clap?* can bring you additional knowledge and insights to heighten your appreciation and empower you to applaud with confidence.

For you who avoid the Three B's of Bach, Beethoven and Brahms, are avowed Motown devotees, Guns'n Roses groupies or Lounge Music lovers, those of you who subscribe to the *bad* descriptions, *When Do I Clap?* will demonstrate that pearls look pretty cool with blue jeans. In other words, Classical music can fit into your life-style and keep you delightfully off balance, giving your life more dimension and fun. The pages that follow will be a top hat and tails striptease, the finale being a great pair of cowboy boots. You **can** relate!

The First Sounds of Music

Below is a Classical music scenario, in which Bill, a Classical music phobic, tries to avoid Bach, Beethoven and Brahms as he goes through his day. You will discover that Bill is relating to Classical music all day long, unwittingly, and is better off for it. Think back: do any of Bill's encounters strike a chord?

> *Bill considers himself a trendy guy. His taste in dress, cars and overall attitude reflect the contemporary view of himself. This modern perspective carries over to his tastes in music. Classical music is not in this category. So, he avoids it. His images of Classical music include people who are snooty, overact and overdress.*
>
> *Anyway, Bill has a free day – no school, no work. There are important errands to do, calls to make, and Classical music has no part in his day.*
>
> *He gets into his car to drive to The Mall, and turns to his favorite vintage rock' n roll station. "Wow, man, Electric Light Orchestra. Cool. 'In the Hall of the Mountain King'," he voices aloud. Then, a nifty commercial about computers: "Neat computer music, real high-tech," he muses.*

The young man arrives at The Mall. Strolling from the parking lot to the heart of the multi-leveled merchandising mecca, he discovers a pianist in a tuxedo playing something kind of jazzy and classy-classical. People are sitting in the surrounding seats, munching on snacks, or just listening. The pianist rises from the bench, and everyone claps in appreciation. Even Bill joins in.

He makes his way to the elevator and ascends to the third level. Conversation mingles with some tight string playing. "Hmm, sounds intense and uplifting," he ponders approvingly.

As Bill strolls along the promenade, he is assaulted by a cacophony of musics: rock from The Gap, flute and harp from Laura Ashley, orchestral from Ralph Lauren, big band from somewhere.

Back in the car, the radio blares out one of his favorites. "All right! Emerson, Lake & Palmer are doing that synthesized trumpet thing," he says out loud, tapping the steering wheel.

Errands done, Bill decides to treat himself and his significant other to a nice dinner. He calls the restaurant, a chic little trattoria named Allegro, and is put on hold. A recording of some guy singing in Italian captivates his attention: "Food must be great here."

As he prepares to go out for the evening, he glances at his watch. "Hm, food for the stomach or food for thought?" His favorite show, William F. Buckley's Firing Line, *will come on while he is out. "I'll tape the show for watching later," he mutters, "that opening music is sophisticated, intense and real intellectual."*

When finally he arrives home late and falls into bed, he is content in the knowledge that he avoided a Classical music confrontation, yet another day.

Or so he thought!

Bill, a classic Classical music phobic, actually has eight encounters in the course of his day. On his car radio, he hears Electric Light Orchestra's *In the Hall of the Mountain King* which was borrowed, synthesized and reinterpreted from a piece of the same name from *Peer Gynt, Suite* No. 1, written in 1888 by the Norwegian composer Edvard Grieg. The computer ad that followed is an excerpt from one of Johann Sebastian Bach's two-part inventions in A minor. Many computer advertisements use Bach's keyboard music.

Inside the Mall, Bill is met by the jazzy strains of George Gershwin's *An American in Paris*. Making his ascent in the elevator, he listens to Franz Schubert's *"Trout" Quintet* in A major – appropriate for small spaces as there are only five instruments playing. It is a light, amusing piece based on a song Schubert wrote about those cunning game fish.

Back in the car and heading for home, Bill's radio blares Emerson, Lake & Palmer's electrified rock interpretation of Aaron Copland's *Fanfare for the Common Man for Brass and Percussion*, written in 1942. On the phone to the restaurant, Bill is put on hold but is treated to Luciano Pavarotti, the celebrated tenor, singing an Italian aria (song) from an Italian opera. It gives an authentic Italian flavor aurally, and promises it gastronomically. The name of the restaurant, Allegro, is an Italian musical term meaning lively, brisk, rapid. It is a popular name for an eating establishment and, hopefully, it reflects the service.

William F. Buckley loves Bach, ergo, setting the dignified, brainy tone for *Firing Line* is the Baroque master's *Brandenburg Concerto No. 2 in F*.

Musical Influences In Our Lives

All Bill, the *classic* Classical music avoider, has to do for inadvertent contact with the likes of Schubert and Gershwin is turn on his car radio, go to the mall, use the phone and click on the television. As stated earlier, Classical excerpts and references permeate our modern media, particularly the Four C's: Commercials, Cartoons, Cinema and Computers.

Commercials

Because advertisers do not have to pay royalties to a vast majority of deceased composers, Classical music as background is a huge money-saver. Even better, it can perfectly reflect the product.

These are some of the most obvious examples:

Snooty –	*Baroque music (1600-1750)*
Amorous –	*Romantic music (19th century)*
High Tech –	*Baroque or 20th century.*

Some types of music lend themselves particularly well to an advertising scenario. This is no accident. There is a kind of music called *Program Music* that tells a story and reflects a mood or a state of mind. At the other end of the spectrum is *Absolute Music* which has no extra-musical connotations, it is simply music for music's sake. Like a chameleon, *Absolute Music* can take on its context creating an association simply by being played simultaneously with a visual advertisement.

To streamline the effect even more to fit the product's image, either *Program* or *Absolute Music* can be arranged for various groups of instruments, it can be sung instead of played, or the theme can be lifted and modified to suit the 30-second time-slot: synthesized, operacized, vocalized and bastardized!

Cartoons

Mickey Mouse, Papa Smurf and Bugs Bunny all have encounters with Classical music. Mickey conducts it, Papa Smurf whistles it, and Bugs even shaves Elmer Fudd's head while singing an aria from *The Barber of Seville*. Disney and Looney Tunes execute the Classics with spare-no-expense orchestration – lush, accurate, consummately professional. It presents an excellent first encounter of Classical music for many children and their parents!

What if hearing *Figaro* conjures up Bugs Bunny impersonating the legendary conductor, Leopold Stokowski? or, if catching the strains of Strauss brings Mickey to mind leading a *Silly Symphony* with the musicians and their instruments airborne? Actually, Saturday mornings are loaded with background music plucked from the Classical repertoire. Watching and listening to the cartoons is a painless way to acquaint the family with the Classics.

Cinema

The ultimate movie cartoon-cum-Classical music is none other than Disney's *Fantasia* (1940). There is a remarkable synergy between music and visuals which rivets the observer of this cinematic masterpiece. The soundtrack was executed by the world-class Philadelphia Orchestra led by Leopold Stokowski. A sequel is in the works.

Disney's *Sleeping Beauty* (1959) is taken from Tchaikovsky's ballet of the same name which is based on the 15th century fairy tale. Much of the original music is even set to words and incorporated into the soundtrack.

The lives of famous and misunderstood composers, frequently embellished, always make for good Hollywood scripts, and they come with ready-made soundtracks. *Rhapsody in Blue* released in 1945, tritely tracks the brief but brilliant 20th century career of George Gershwin. *Amadeus,* released in 1984, brings a misunderstood Mozart into the mainstream, and not only with it creates more demand for recordings of the soundtrack, but also for all the musical output of this genius of the Classical period. *Immortal Beloved* (1995) tracks the fictional account of Beethoven's love life.

When used as a thematic device to reflect or enhance action or an emotion, Classical music can be an extremely powerful tool. The film, *Platoon* (1986) effectively uses 20th century composer Samuel Barber's *Adagio for Strings* to mirror the horrific Vietnam war experience. In *The Age of Innocence* (1993), Beethoven's *Adagio Cantabile* from his 1797/98 *Sonata No. 8 in C Minor* (known as the Pathétique) simmers along with the emotions of the two entangled main characters. Both are *Adagios* (slow movements) yet they reflect disparate emotions. The first is used as a death theme, the second, a love theme.

Computers

A great deal of software, particularly directed at children, features music by the no-pay-royalty masters. On one program, if a child works through a math problem successfully, he or she will hear the rapid-fire theme from the opening of Mozart's *Symphony No. 40*. Another program rewards a good deed with the same composer's *Eine Kleine Nachtmusik*. It is fun to hear a seven-year old enthusiastically hum these themes; they hold a positive, educational association. One day, when those little computer whizzes take their seats in a concert hall, they will already have a rapport with the music.

Music has been documented for over sixteen centuries. It does not suddenly appear with Bach in the late 17th century and vanish with Mahler in the early 20th century. By circa 300 A.D. the monks of the Catholic Church were already inking notations onto manuscripts in the interest of standardizing the use of music for religious services. In another five hundred years, a more formal system begins to emerge governing how church chants should be composed. The language and notation of that early music co-evolved, leading to our current mechanics of notation, and ultimately, to traditional harmony nearly one thousand years later. Traditional harmony is a compositional Rosetta Stone upon which all American and European music is based even to this day in Rock, Blues, Jazz, New Age and Country.

But rules are made to be stretched and tested. Composers became bolder about toying with and, eventually, redefining traditional harmony. A climax was reached in the 20th century when notes were again reorganized, and traditional harmony was challenged by offering a daring alternative. But, take heart, those of you who have difficulty understanding 20th century music; traditional harmony, as previously stated, still prevails, not only in the Top 40, on television, in nursery rhymes and in musical theater but also in Classical music. So, there is no need to shy away from concerts. You may even enjoy contemporary music, the traditional as well as the outrageous.

In spite of all this refining, there is a common thread that connects the earliest forms and language of music to what is being commissioned today by orchestra and opera. It weaves all these colorful pieces into one tapestry called Classical music.

What is Classical Music anyway?

In its broadest sense, the term, Classical music, is used generically to describe an organized and structured level of music composed in the European tradition, in contrast to popular or folk/ethnic music. This spans a good part of Western history through the present day: from Medieval Gregorian chants to a 1993 opera by Ezra Laderman called *Marilyn* (yes, Monroe), presented by the New York City Opera Company, and beyond.

The term also refers to a specific historical period, called the *Classical* period which occurred roughly between 1750 and 1825, centered in and around the city of Vienna. Haydn, Mozart and Beethoven epitomize this music.

Classical music is traditionally divided into six historical periods: Middle Ages (300-1425), Renaissance (1425-1600), Baroque (1600-1750), Classical (1750-1825), Romantic (1825-1910), and 20th Century (1910-1999).

Music from the four most recent periods fills the majority of concert programs. Symphonic or opera seasons rely heavily on the music of the 19th century. However, all four of these recent periods of music are full of masterpieces which universally appeal to audiences, who want to hear them over and over again.

Now that you are tuned in to how Classical music is already a part of your daily life, why not consciously add it into the mix of work and play? Here are several ideas:

- Whistle Beethoven's *Fifth Symphony* while you pull weeds or shovel show. The task will go more quickly. Maybe you will recall the theme being set to a disco beat for the 1977 movie, *Saturday Night Fever,* re-emerging as a No. 1 Chart Record called "A Fifth of Beethoven".

- Watch a toddler instinctively dance with joy to the exuberant strains of Vivaldi's *Mandolin Concerto in C Major.* It may conjure up a visual of a large real estate company's television ads.

- Jog around the track or work out at the gym to Copland's ballet, *Rodeo*. The miles and pounds will melt away. You may have a sudden craving for beef since it has been used in a television spot promoting it as being "what's for dinner".

Keep your ears open! You never know where you might run into Bach, or Vivaldi, or Verdi, or Strauss, or Glass, or Anonymous, or Hermannus Contractus, or Bartok, or Glinka, or Liszt, or Wagner, or Haydn, or Mozart, or Gershwin, or...or...or....

Movement 1

"So, When DO I Clap?"

"Why doesn't anybody go to concerts any more?...because the halls are full of people like you!...Half asleep, nodding and smiling, ... hawking and spitting into paper bags...just a nice back-ground murmur of wheezing, belching, intestinal gurgles, scratching, sucking, croaking, an entire opera house crammed full of them."

Thomas Pynchon
Gravity's Rainbow (1973)

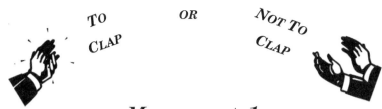

TO   OR   NOT TO
CLAP   CLAP

Movement 1

So, When DO I Clap?

The simple reality is that many people would rather have a root-canal than be faced with the dilemma of when to clap at a concert or opera.

As a result, they do one of two things: they go to a performance and are haunted about applauding and do not even *hear* the music; or they stay home, missing out on the thrill of a live concert.

For those who have braved the concert hall, there is the occasional dark moment when a group of music lovers breaks into applause between movements (sections) of a piece, interrupting the concentration of the musicians. Unfortunately, this inspires the wrath of some conductors or ensembles. In the early 1990s one such incident occurred during a concert in which Isaac Stern, Emanuel Ax, Yo-Yo Ma and Jaime Laredo were playing Beethoven. Some of the audience applauded after the rousing first movement. Mr. Stern slowly turned in his chair, faced the audience and scowled at them, pointing his violin bow in a threatening manner. As a result, people were afraid to clap even when the piece was over. Certainly, the experience colored their perception of the music, and probably scared a few right out of the concert hall for good.

However, most conductors and musicians are more gracious about errant applause. They will turn to the audience and say "thank you" and will instruct the people to *wait until the very end of the piece.* After all, knowing when to clap is not exactly a genetic instinct. Chances are that someone in that audience is there for the first time. At one time or another, everyone has been swept along by the music and felt compelled to celebrate its excellence by putting one hand against the other.

Mis-timed applause is just the tip of the iceberg as far as ways the audience finds to subvert the entranced state of the performers. As experienced concert- and opera-goers know – and which you are about to find out – there is more than one performance being played out in the concert hall. The *Symphony In The Seats* is an audience-generated, non-musical phenomenon which, at times, can give even a hundred-strong orchestra fierce competition. Perhaps, even you may have performed one or more of these selections:

Symphony In The Seats

"THE FIREDOOR SUITE"

> Ever popular, this is usually heard just after the start of the program and recurs after intermission when the ushers have been outsmarted by latecomers. It is characterized by the slamming of heavy, concert hall doors.

"THE COUGHING CANTATA"

> This selection is prevalent during flu season, as is *"The Sneezing Sonata"*, both of which accompany the music's quietest, most magical moments. Many performing groups now provide cough drops for the audience to quell the cacophony.

"WRAPPERSODY"

> To alleviate the symptoms of the two preceding works, the audience often crackles its way through this number.

"POPS"

Chewing gum is its recurring theme.

"SQUEAKY SEAT SUITE"

This is the result of constant, restless shifting.

"FOOT-TAPPING TOCCATA"

A lively beat from the stage is the inspiration.

"AIR-HEAD ARIA"

It consists of wildly jerking head motion, and is a characteristic of air-conducting.

"FRANTIC INTERLUDE"

This piece is characterized by a mad dash of females out of the hall just before the end of the act or first half, in order to be first in line at the restroom.

"SHOPPING BAGATELLE"

A staple at the Friday matinee, it features Bergdorf's, Saks, Macy's, The Gap, and that famous duet, Lord & Taylor.

"KEY-RING CYCLE"

This is heard toward the end of the program in anticipation of mass vehicular departure.

No-Faux Insurance

Whenever several hundred human beings – or even just several – assemble under one roof, there will always be distractions. When these people are supposed to sit quietly for at least an hour concentrating intently on the music-making before them, distractions will be ever-present. But, here are some suggestions which, if you stick to them, will ensure the conductor will not stop and hurl his baton – javelin-style – at you, or that your fellow audience members will not bind and gag you with your own candy wrappers and gold chains.

The most distracting accessory at a concert or opera is the electronic device. It all started with the digital watch, modulated to pagers/beepers and has cadenced to cellular phones. Leave them home. If you must carry a beeper, leave it with the box office personnel and tell them where you are sitting.

Cameras of any kind and recording equipment are strictly forbidden in most concert situations.

Many in our population have need of wearing hearing aids. Please be mindful of the piercing pitch these devices can give off if not adjusted properly. An example: During the 1993-94 season at Lincoln Center at a performance given by the New York Philharmonic, an unfortunate and inadvertent disruption occurred. After the first movement of Rachmaninoff's *Symphonic Dances*, guest conductor, Leonard Slatkin, turned around to the audience and announced that someone had "an electronic device" that was disturbing the musicians, as well as the audience. It turned out to be a hearing aid. Before continuing, the maestro lightly added: "It wasn't in the right key." Everyone chuckled, the situation was resolved, and the concert ended swimmingly.

Other unwelcome audience percussives, which have been around for centuries, include noisy jewelry. Ladies, why do you think those bracelets are called *bangles*?

And while we are on the subject of female finery, please remember to leave the grand chapeau at home and do not fluff your hairdo, too. Both obstruct *le view!* Which rhymes with "pee-yew"! Save the "Obsession" fragrance (perfume) for another venue – it may trigger someone's sneezing fit at twenty paces in every direction – Ah-CHEW! And before cold weather sets in, air out coats and clothing that have been curing in mothballs. EEW!

If you are worried about what to wear, do not be. Generally, people are not dressing as formally for a musical event as they once did. The only time you might see a tuxedo or long evening gown is on Opening Night, or for a special gala benefit. The invitation will indicate "Black Tie". People do tend to dress up more in large cosmopolitan cities for evening events: usually coat and tie for the men and informal outfits or nice pant-suits for the ladies. In the suburbs events are a bit more relaxed, but coat and tie are still very much in evidence on weekend evenings. For matinee performances, dress has loosened up even more. If the program is part of a summer festival, casual is the rule as most families spread out on a lawn with a picnic. And if the show is for kids, anything goes!

If you do plan to dine out prior to a performance whether on the grass or in a restaurant, allow enough time. Lugging the picnic basket, lawn chairs and other paraphernalia from the car, setting up, enjoying the repast, cleaning up after, and – if you have reserved seats – getting to the concert area – you will need to allow two hours. For an 8:30 curtain, for example, arrive at the picnic grounds or make a restaurant reservation for no later than 6:30. Take into consideration traveling time, parking and picking up your tickets at the box office, if you have not obtained them beforehand.

Remember, you are what you eat! And smoke! And drink! Go easy on the cocktails and wine – you do not want your head bobbing like a cork during the concert. And finally, consider a visit to the restroom just before you leave the restaurant. Lines at the concert hall are always serpentine and sluggish, particularly for the ladies room. There are times it is so bad that women dash into the relatively empty men's room.

With the sartorial, temporal and gastronomical dilemmas resolved, aim to be in your seat fifteen minutes before curtain time. This seems to be the right amount of time for getting settled, which includes calming down after dealing with traffic, babysitters, the subway, dining and all the stresses of your life from which you want to escape for the next hour or two. If you are late, the ushers will not allow you to be seated until there is a break in the music, such as the end of a movement or a piece, or maybe even an entire act!

In Your Seat

Now, it is fifteen minutes to curtain! Just as the musicians are readying themselves for the concert, you also need to make a few preparations to avoid causing a disturbance during the performance.

Whatever items you anticipate needing while in your seat, get them out now: eyeglasses, breath mints, hard candy, cough drops, chewing gum (unwrap all of these and put them in a pocket or a tissue). Blow your nose, fix your hair, adjust your hearing aid, wiggle one last time – do whatever you have to do to get comfortable.

Once settled, open your program and read, at least, the notes about the first selection so you will know what to listen for. This is especially important if you are attending an opera which often is sung in Italian, German, French or some language other than English; the story line is usually explained in the program.

A typical program contains the following: a page listing trustees, officers and administrators; a list of volunteers; profiles of the conductor/musical director, guest soloist(s), or singers; program notes about the works to be performed and the composers; a list of orchestra members; advertisements; advance notices of upcoming events; and finally, smack in the middle of the book, the program page.

The program page tells you, in order, what selections the orchestra will perform or list the acts and settings, if an opera. Sample of a symphony program will be found on page 19.

Do not be intimidated by those foreign words and strange terms! Relax, you will catch on. Opus numbers (i.e. Opus 5) only indicate the order of publication of a composer's works. Such terms as *Adagio*, *Andante*, *Allegro* and *Presto* are merely conventional designations of speed at which a movement should be played – from very slow to very fast. Terms such as *Scherzo*, *Fugue*, *Sonata* or *Concerto* are forms of music. (Musical terms mentioned here are further described in the last chapter entitled "Help Me, Rondo!" , The Glossary, of this book.)

THE CLEVELAND ORCHESTRA
CHRISTOPH VON DOHNÁNYI • MUSIC DIRECTOR

1999-2000 PROGRAM 1
SEVERANCE HALL

Thursday evening, September 23, 1999, at 8:00 p.m.
Friday evening, September 24, 1999, at 8:00 p.m.
Saturday evening, September 25, 1999, at 8:00 p.m.

Christoph von Dohnányi, *conductor*

THOMAS ADÈS
(b. 1971)

Asyla

MAURICE RAVEL
(1875-1937)

Piano Concerto in G major

Allegramente
Adagio assai
Presto

EMANUEL AX, *piano*

INTERMISSION

PIOTR ILYICH TCHAIKOVSKY
(1840-1893)

**Symphony No. 6 ("Pathétique")
in B minor, Op. 74**

Adagio — Allegro non troppo
Allegro con grazia
Allegro molto vivace
Finale: Adagio lamentoso

These concerts are sponsored by The Cleveland Foundation.

Emanuel Ax's appearance with The Cleveland Orchestra
is made possible by a contribution to the Orchestra's Guest Artist Fund
from the late Dr. Frank Hovorka in honor of Dorothy Humel Hovorka.

The concerts will end at about 10:25 p.m.

CONCERT PREVIEW (in the Concert Hall beginning one hour before each concert):
"Meet the Artist" with Emanuel Ax in conversation with Thomas W. Morris,
Exeuctive Director of The Cleveland Orchestra

REPRINTED COURTESY OF THE CLEVELAND ORCHESTRA
SAMPLE SYMPHONY PROGRAM

At the Symphony Orchestra

The symphony orchestra concert, if you are unfamiliar with it, can be an intimidating experience. Most of the time, the musicians are decked out in formal attire. With seemingly throngs of them wielding all sorts of instruments, it looks like a big confusing private party up on stage – to which you were not invited.

BUT YOU WERE! *You bought a ticket.* They are all there **for you**. More importantly, you and the orchestra are both there for the music.

John G. Ross

BOSTON SYMPHONY ORCHESTRA

The Visuals

The modern-day symphony orchestra varies in size from thirty to one hundred musicians, depending on the music's requirements. Daunting to the unacquainted eye, the orchestra consists of only four sections:

STRINGS

WOODWINDS

BRASS

PERCUSSION

The STRINGS are located in the front of the orchestra. Between sixty and seventy violins, violas, cellos and double basses (pronounced like bases) make up this section.

Directly in the center behind the strings are the fourteen to eighteen WOODWINDS: piccolos, flutes, oboes, English horn, clarinets, bass clarinet, bassoons and contrabassoon.

Due to their relative loudness, the BRASSES bring up the rear: trumpets, French horns, trombones and tuba.

Up to six PERCUSSIONISTS and at the very least, one timpanist, are usually situated at the left rear of the stage (sometimes the timpani will be at the center rear): cymbals, snare drum, bass drum, timpani, chimes, marimba, bells, xylophone, triangle and other rhythm-makers.

When called for, a harp, piano, organ, celeste or harpsichord will be positioned off to the side of the orchestra (except in a piano/harpsichord concerto which features the instrument, in which case it is placed immediately to the left of the conductor).

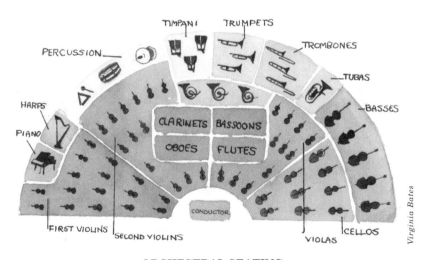

ORCHESTRAL SEATING

The word symphony comes from the Greek word, *symphonia* meaning *sounding together*. Eventually the term came to refer to an instrumental ensemble without voices. By the 19th century, the word meant an orchestral composition in three to five distinct movements.

In the 18th century, Haydn and Mozart epitomized the Classical symphony in four movements. But Beethoven and the subsequent Romantic composers pushed the form to new limits, calling for a wider selection of instruments, but still for the most part retaining the four-movement format.

A movement is a section of a piece. Even though it may sound conclusive, it is part of a whole as conceived by the composer.

Therefore, clap at the end of the entire piece, which may have several movements, never between movements. *At this point the conductor turns away from the orchestra and completely faces the audience wearing a happily exhausted expression.*

Symphony orchestras also often play overtures or tone poems which may be one-movement works – there is no question when to clap here. But the *concerto* is another matter.

The concerto is a piece, usually in three movements, which features a soloist (or sometimes a duet) playing along as equal partner with the orchestra. A special characteristic of the concerto is something called a cadenza, which can sometimes confuse the concert-goer.

A cadenza is a flashy virtuoso passage occurring near the end of a movement which affords the solo instrumentalist an opportunity to show off his talent, following which orchestra and soloist combine their energies to finish the movement out together. **The best advice is not to clap until you know the final movement is ended.**

The Rituals

As the musicians meander onto the stage or settle into the pit, a series of rapidly-moving rituals ensues. The orchestra warms up until the concertmaster enters. The principal first violinist is the most important member of the orchestra, and sits directly to the left of the conductor. A signal is made to the principal (head) oboe to play the note "A" to which the orchestra tunes, or an "A" is struck on the piano if one is to be used.

When everyone is tuned, the conductor enters, sometimes with a guest soloist, and shakes hands with the concertmaster. With an energetic, adrenaline-spurred leap onto the podium, the conductor nods to the orchestra, waits for things to settle down (on stage and *in the audience*), raises his baton and the performance begins.

Applause is an integral part of these rituals. Here are some of the specific times to clap at a symphony orchestra concert:

When the concertmaster enters. *He or she is the leader of the first violin section – a great honor.*

When the conductor enters.

When the guest soloist enters. *Orchestras often feature guest musicians or singers.*

At the conclusion of an ENTIRE **piece.**

When the conductor re-enters after the intermission.

When the conductor exits and reappears. *Keep clapping until the conductor reaches the destination: be it podium or wings.*

At the conclusion of an encore. *When shouted, "Encore!" means "Again!" and refers to a piece added or repeated at the audience's behest.*

At the Chamber Music Concert

The chamber music concert is similar to an orchestral concert in that much of the repertoire has the same forms. In other words, *movements*.

The big difference is in the number of musicians on stage. Where a symphony orchestra can have a roster of fifty to one hundred, the chamber orchestra would have a maximum of around thirty musicians.

Chamber music is written for small ensembles, such as duets, trios, quartets, quintets, sextets, septets, octets and nonets, to name a few. It is performed in a smaller venue than the vast concert hall, in a place such as a church, library or recital hall.

 Unlike a symphony orchestra concert where the musicians meander onto the stage and take their seats to no applause, **it is appropriate to clap when a small ensemble makes its entrance.**

It is essential not to applaud between movements at this type of concert, as the entire flavor is one of intimacy and intense concentration.

At the Solo Recital

The solo recital is a concert given by one performer alone, or by one who plays an instrument or sings and is usually accompanied by a pianist. The program is designed to display the performer's mastery of the instrument as well as his or her artistry, musicianship and expressive talent. The most popular kinds of solo recitals are: piano solo, voice-piano, violin-piano, cello-piano, woodwind-piano, and solo string. Frequently performed literature for the instrumental solo recital includes sonatas and suites, but there are numerous other types of pieces.

 It is important never to clap between the movements of a piece.

For a voice recital, the audience must take special care because of a phenomenon called **The Song Cycle.** *This is a collection of technically and artistically linked components (songs) which must never be interrupted.*

Clapping between these songs would be akin to breaking a string of pearls.

Again, follow the program.

At the Choral Concert

The choral concert features a chorus of mixed (soprano, alto, tenor, baritone and bass), all-male or all-female voices. Sometimes there is instrumental accompaniment ranging from a full-blown orchestra to that of a small ensemble, or simply an organ or piano. Very often, it is *a cappella* or unaccompanied.

Forms of choral music most often performed are: cantata, oratorio, Mass and Requiem. All are religious in nature, the exception being the earliest cantatas which were secular. Cantatas are shorter than oratorios. An *oratorio* is an extended musical dramatic work consisting of numerous sections. A *Mass* is the five-section musical service of the Roman Catholic Church. A *Requiem* is a multi-movement Mass for the Dead.

Clap when the choral director turns completely around with that "We did it!" look on his face.

As always, there are exceptions. At the popular *Messiah Sing-In* at Lincoln Center in New York City, audience members – who sing along with the choruses while guest performers take the arias and recitatives – scream and yell as though they were at a rock concert after they complete the sensational *Hallelujah Chorus* by Handel. And then they sing it again!

So, use your better judgment. One cannot help but think that Mr. Handel is smiling down on Lincoln Center during those sing-ins.

At the Early Music Concert

Audiences are less familiar with these types of concerts as they are not nearly as prevalent as those mentioned above. But more and more people are discovering this lively and important music. As a result, more concerts, and even whole festivals, devoted to this early genre are proliferating.

A recent trend in performance has been to recreate music to sound the way it did when it was written. This is achieved through the use of authentic, old instruments or reproductions, using the performance practices of the period. It is called *Period Performance*.

For music written before the 19th century, conductors as we know them did not exist. (That did not happen until Felix Mendelssohn stepped in "with a white stick" and led a group of musicians in London.) The ensembles took their cues from the harpsichordist or first violinist or from some other musician.

 The best advice one can give regarding an early music concert is to follow the program carefully and **clap at the end of a multi-movement piece**.

At the Opera

In the 18th and 19th centuries, opera singers typically hired groups of people for the express purpose of sitting in the audience and clapping during that singer's performance. They were called *claques*. They whipped up the audience and (hopefully) the press, helping to advance that singer's career.

Considered a huge *faux pas* these days, nevertheless, one can still on occasion discern a singer's enthused entourage in an opera house audience, by the "Bravo" (for a male singer), "Bravi" (for an ensemble), or "Brava" (for a female) shouted histrionically at the end of the number. They are usually the ones who jump to their feet making the rest of the audience feel sheepish and therefore coercing them to rise as well. It is a tacky practice.

Anyway, opera is a different animal from the concert. In terms of clapping, it is more closely related to the musical production of the Broadway variety. Opera combines the resources of the orchestra with the singers (not to mention the stage and costume designers). Its main ingredients are the overture (an opening piece for orchestra), the recitative (an introductory vocal solo declaiming the narrative), the aria (a song-like piece for vocal soloist), and the ensemble piece (anything from a duet to a chorus). Most of the operas regularly performed today were written from the time of Mozart to the present.

Ergo: **Clap at the end of each act.**

There is one huge exception to this rule. Richard Wagner's *Parsifal* was conceived on the subject of Good Friday and is regarded by many as a religious rite when performed.

Do NOT clap at the end of Act I in particular, or

you will be promptly (and emphatically) shushed.

Here is a list of additional times when clapping is welcome at the opera, unless otherwise specified by management:

When the conductor makes his entrance.

Sometimes when the curtain goes up, but not always. *Clapping here or refraining from doing so is not an indicator of the audience's opinion of the set design. It simply depends on the opera and the mood.*

When a superstar makes an entrance.

At the end of a sensationally-sung aria (solo).

At the end of a sensationally-sung ensemble piece.

And finally, whether you are at an opera, the symphony or an elementary school piano recital in the teacher's living room, here are two more important pointers:

Do not even think of talking during the performance, *and*

Never get up and leave during the music unless it is a dire emergency.

Now that you know when to clap – among other things – sit back, relax, close your eyes and let the **music** – not your **fears** – overwhelm your **senses**!

Movement 2

But First, A Word About Early Music

"Music is a science that would have us laugh and sing and dance."

Guillaume de Machaut
14th Century French composer

Movement 2

But First, A Word About Early Music

Contrary to what many Classical music radio stations, record stores and concert series may lead the music-lover to believe, Classical music did not suddenly appear on New Year's Day, 1600 (the Music 101 date for the beginning of the Baroque period). Classical music, as well as cathedrals, were going through a period of construction. The idea of reaching towards heaven was a driving force of not only the church but also stone masons, architects and composers.

From about 300 A.D. Gregorian Chant, Medieval and Renaissance music led up to that revered year. And in the Dark Ages preceding the Renaissance – as far as music was concerned – it was anything but "**Dark**".

While architects and stone masons reached for the heavens by constructing cathedrals, their musical counterparts, composers, strove for the same purpose. They wrote structured music for the Catholic Mass in Western Europe to resound within

Photodisc

**BRUNELLESCHI'S DOME, 1436
CATHEDRAL OF FLORENCE,**

those magnificent structures. This activity began in monastic centers and then continued in the great cities where universities were the focus of scholarly life.

Beyond the walls of higher learning, there existed a large body of colorful (off-color, actually) secular music, such as the music sung in the fields and taverns by the unlearned. In an example of unprecedented compositional ingenuity involving the spiritual interacting with the earthly, medieval composers turned to this rich source of common man's music as a foundation for readily-accessible religious music.

In fact, those folk tunes were so singable that "serious" composers took advantage of them and integrated the melodies *and the lyrics* into a musical setting of the Catholic Mass. While musically, it was an important innovation that one theme – the tavern ditty as it were – appeared in each of the five sections of the Mass therefore uniting it melodically, it sounded something like taking *Ninety-nine Bottles of Beer on the Wall*, giving it to the tenor voice, and adding a soprano and bass with religious text around it. You might hear the words *Deum* and *beer* sung simultaneously.

But the Council of Trent (1545-1563), an assembly of the church powers which ruled on matters of discipline and doctrine, put a stop to this economical practice of recycling the secular as the sacred (it probably packed the cathedral, and everyone hummed along as they had the night before in the pub)! Composers had to come up with their own themes, or borrow something more respectable than the equivalent of a college fight song. They left the main melody with the tenor voice. This was called *cantus firmus*. Around this framework the soprano, bass and other voices were built.

Construction was on nearly everyone's mind, with the cathedrals rising slowly towards the firmament. The concerns of stone masons and architects paralleled those of composers, namely proportion and symmetry.

A great example of manipulation of proportion affecting melody and rhythm occurs in a work by the Burgundian Guillaume Dufay, in a type of piece called a *motet*: **a sacred, polyphonic choral composition**. Written for the dedication of Brunelleschi's dome of the Cathedral of Florence in 1436, *Nuper rosarum flores* is extraordinary in that it contains the exact same overall proportions, rhythmically, that the dome has, architecturally. This is no accident: composer and architect collaborated to create a structural and aural wonder!

While you may not hear Dufay's motet on the airwaves, Early music has been making inroads into our popular culture, particularly the Gregorian chant. Characterized by a single male voice which took advantage of the slow reverberations of the great cathedrals and monasteries, or voices in unison, this type of chant codified around 600 A.D., thanks to Pope Gregory I. Who would have guessed, then, that a recording by the Benedictine Monks of Santo Domingo de Filos – a Spanish monastic order – would fly out of record stores because listeners found it mesmerizing, other-worldly and soothing (and the *New York Times* loved it)! The haunting, spiritual quality of chant was seized upon by advertising agencies who made it sensual by underpinning it with a slow sultry drum beat. In some instances, the men's voices have been replaced by women's, giving the chant yet another ethereal spin. On your radio, you may hear music by a group call Enigma, which is labeled as a Gregorian chant techno-band. The group specializes in blending chant with electronic, booming dance music primarily for dance clubs. A religious experience? Amen!

Film makers in recent years in the quest for authenticity, have finally figured out that a period film somehow misses with a 20th Century sound track. The collection of keyboard music of the 16th century anthology called *The Fitzwilliam Virginal Book* is frequently heard behind milk maidens and musketeers. It is also easier today to find musicians trained in the performance of Early music, sometimes on authentic instruments or at the very least on those faithfully reproduced.

Michael Praetorius, Syntagma Musicum

EARLY TRIO PLAYING SACKBUT INSTRUMENTS

Around the holidays, Early music is the preferred soundtrack: evocative of quintessential Noels and other ancient celebrations. A few seconds into the CD and you have caught the spirit.

Why is Early music so compelling? Because it is the tangible ancestor whose lineage we can trace and whose traits we recognize today in our own music. It is charming and basic and accessible but deliciously ancient in its pre-tonal language and unbridled rhythms. Although Early music is highly complex structurally, it sometimes sounds refreshingly naive to our modern, conditioned ears. It is familiar in a comfortingly archaic way: an antidote to present-day cacophony.

But thirteen hundred years is an enormous time span for one designation of Early music, particularly when you consider that the Classical period of Haydn, Mozart and Beethoven lasted only seventy-five years. It helps, however, that Early music can be broken down into Medieval and Renaissance periods.

Chronological Highlights:

I. Medieval

300-900 A.D.

Monks throughout Western Europe composed what became known as *Gregorian Chant,* named after Gregory I who was Pope from 590 to 604 and who standardized church music.

> *Gregorian Chant is a single-line melody sung in Latin by unaccompanied male voices. It has an ethereal, other-worldly quality.*

Ninth Century

A type of early *polyphony,* called *organum,* was developed in which **two or more independent melodies were composed within one composition**. In the earliest examples **the two voices are parallel to one another**, but over time they become more independent.

Tenth and Eleventh Centuries

Composers in these two centuries relied on eight Church Modes, which were eight-note scales differentiated by the arrangement of their whole and half steps. For example, the third or Phrygian Mode, which begins on the note, E, progresses EFGABCDE. If you look at the keys on a piano, you will see that there is no black key between E and F, and B and C. These are called *half-steps*. Between all the others are whole steps. It is this pattern of half-step, whole, whole, whole, half-step and whole which distinguishes this mode from the seven other steps. These scales led towards the tonalities of major and minor keys in the 1600s.

Liturgical Dramas enjoyed popularity in Europe. **They were based on stories dramatized from the Bible and were initially sung in Latin.** Later, they were mixed with local language. They had dialogue and action.

Big breakthrough! Guido d'Arrezzo invented a four-line staff complete with notes and clefs, the precursor to the present-day five-line staff. He also comes up with a system to teach singing – literally by hand – called *solmization*. His system evolved into a method of teaching scales and intervals by syllables, such as *do* (originally ut), *re, mi, fa, sol*, and *si (or ti)* – each syllable is assigned to its own joint or fingertip.

Twelfth Century

Ah yes, it was a good time to be an aristocrat. In France you could be a *Troubadour* in the south or if from the north, a *Trouvère*. If you were German, a *Minnesinger*. **All three were poet-musicians who composed and performed songs about courtly love.** They went from castle to castle entertaining the elite and their guests.

In Marcabru's *"L'autrier jost' una sebissa"*, a pastorela, the Troubadour sings about his efforts to seduce a peasant girl:

He begins:

> *The other day by a hedge-row*
> *I found a lowly shepherdess,*
> *Full of joy and good sense.*
> *She was the daughter of a coun-*
> *   try woman...*

and concludes with *her* response:

> *Sir, the owl warns you:*
> *This one gapes at the painting,*
> *Another waits for manna.*

In other words, "No way, Jose!"

Thirteenth Century

On the sacred side, the *motet* was in its embryonic stage. In its infancy, it was a short piece for two or three voices, but later on it became longer, more fully developed and complicated. It was frequently written in two languages, French and Latin – bilingual texts. The greatest motet composers were active in the Renaissance: from Flanders, Ockeghem and Obrecht; Josquin des Prez from France; Palestrina in Italy; and Tallis in England.

In the last century of Medieval music, rhythm has become regulated and formally organized into set patterns.

Fourteenth Century

During this century there was a transitional period known as the *Ars Nova* (new art) in France and Italy. At the powerful and widely influential court in the Burgundian section of France, the most brilliant composer was Guillaume de Machaut, who wrote the first complete setting of the Ordinary of the Mass.

In Northern Italy, the *madrigal* was evolving. **It began as a vocal composition, based on a poem, for two or three voices.** This early madrigal bears no relation to the 16th century English madrigal which was written in an intensely contrapuntal style, that is, two or more melodies heard simultaneously.

II. The Renaissance

Fifteenth and Sixteenth Centuries

The Flemish, the Dutch and the Burgundians dominated the musical world, turning out high-quality compositions:

the Italians were known for beautiful melodies;

the French, for their logic in musical construction;

and the English, for their richness of harmony.

Taken together, Renaissance music is a rich blend of beauty and intellectualism.

An ideal Renaissance concert program would include works by the following composers who were the most important and innovative of the time: Guillaume Dufay, Johannes Ockeghem, Josquin des Prez, Giovanni Pierluigi da Palestrina, Orlando di Lasso, John Dunstable, William Byrd and Giovanni Gabrieli.

The most common musical forms in which these composers plied their craft were masses, motets, madrigals and settings for secular lyric poetry such as the *chanson* in France and in Italy the *frottola*, the *canzona* and the *ricercare* – a piece distinguished by imitative treatment of one or more themes, similar to the jazz of the 20th Century. These musical forms reigned supreme in the instrumental music category.

Within these forms, composers carried over the architectural aspects of music from their Medieval predecessors – again, proportion and symmetry. Composers also infused their music with symbolism, word-painting, hidden meanings – extra-musical phenomena yet inherent, essential to the whole. Music was both micro- and macro-cosmically conceived.

Nowhere is the Renaissance cross-pollination of various and seemingly disparate disciplines more epitomized than in a study group formed in late 16th century Florence. Called a *camerata,* it consisted of a group of intellectuals who gathered to discuss the arts. What resulted musically, was *monody*: **a single voice with an accompaniment of static chords**. Gone was the cluttered counterpoint, the linear thinking. The voice, the MELODY was the thing. Theatrically, the *camerata*'s combination of music, poetry and science led to an early form of opera originally called *dramma per musica*, or "drama by means of music." Later, the term, *opera,* came into use in Italian, meaning "work".

Italian composer, Claudio Monteverdi (circa1567-1643), picked up where the *camerata* left off. A transitional figure whose work went in one era and out the next (the Baroque), Monteverdi is best known for his operas *Orfeo* (1607) and *Arianna* (1608), epitomizing the new focus on the voice, "showing the monody", as it were.

Early Technology

The new music had exposure as never before, thanks to the enormous strides made in printing. While Johann Gutenberg perfected the art of printing books with moveable type around 1450, it was Ottaviano de Petrucci in Venice who, by 1523, had published fifty-nine volumes of music using moveable type. This method spread to other parts of Europe.

Bringing the printed notes to life were ancestors of today's instruments. Some of them had amusingly bizarre names, such as sackbuts which are Renaissance trombones.

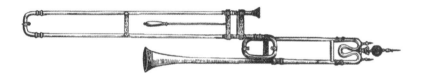

The virginal was an early keyboard with plucked strings.

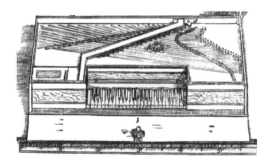

Viols were gut-stringed instruments played with bows.

Recorders were flutes with whistle-like mouthpieces...

and lutes were guitar-like stringed instruments.

Later, keyboard instruments included the clavichord and the harpsichord. There were also organs, harps, zithers, trumpets, flutes, bagpipes and an assortment of noisemakers such as bells, drums and tambourines.

On these instruments and with their voices, Medieval and Renaissance musicians performed primarily in churches and castles. Formal concerts did not make a documented appearance until the 1600s. Surely, outside the cathedral walls appreciative listeners applauded after a rousing number. Then again, a freshly laid egg hurled at the performer's lute might have been the response to a mediocre presentation.

Overall, in these thirteen hundred years there was a drive toward tonality – our current system of major and minor keys. Like their 20th century counterparts, Early music composers sought a new order, constantly experimenting, striving for perfection – landing on a method, then moving on. Within their stepping stone regimens, Early music composers came up with music of great eloquence, emotion and best of all, humor. Some say it was a dark, unenlightened time, and in a way composers were groping through their music. Thanks to them, however, voilà, the Baroque.

Early Listening

Music of the Middle Ages and the Renaissance is usually lumped into an *Early Music* category in record stores. There you may find all types of collections: instrumental, vocal, sacred, secular and by region. You will find dances and dompes, masses, motets, madrigals; all types of gimmicky CD titles, too. From "Saints and Sinners" to Anonymous 4", to a group who calls itself "Mystical Madrigal Tour". Let your curiosity be piqued. Here are some suggestions to help guide you through this marketing maze.

Medieval:

Gregorian Chant

Songs by Troubadours, Trouvères and Minnesingers

Works by:

Guillaume de Machaut

Francesco Landini

Renaissance:

John Dunstable

Guillaume Dufay

Missa l'homme armé

Johannes Ockeghem

Josquin des Prez

motet: *Ave Maria*

Giovanni Pierluigi da Palestrina

William Byrd

Mass for Four Voices

Mass for Five Voices

In felix ego

Movement 3

The Stock Baroquers:
Bach, Handel, Vivaldi & Company

"A good composer should be able to set public notices to music."

Georg Phillipp Telemann
1681-1767

JOHANN SEBASTIAN BACH

Movement 3

The Stock Baroquers:
Bach, Handel, Vivaldi & Company

In the 20th century, music of this period is accused of being *Muzak for the Intelligentsia*.

And advertisers, retailers, Wall Street and restaurants all cash in on its appeal to the educated and enlightened class.

Baroque music can give snob appeal to mustard, a computer, a subcompact Japanese car (reverse snobbism) and even a taxicab ride. With Bach in the background, *haute cuisine* is enhanced in a restaurant. Shopping is more civilized when Handel reaches you through the racks. The skies seem friendlier because Vivaldi's music plays in your ear when the ticket agent puts you on hold.

You may not know who composed the music you hear and enjoy, but chances are, if it is Baroque, it is one of the Stock Baroquers: Bach, Handel or Vivaldi.

Advertising whizzes have been onto it since the 1980s; there is something about this music that grabs you and never offends you, that sounds smart without being condescending, and that you can have in the background either in the office or in the kitchen all day long and still be happy.

Baroque music thrived in Europe from around 1600 to 1750, with the Italian and German regions being the centers of activity. In France, Louis XIV was on the throne, in America the pilgrims landed at Plymouth Rock, and Oliver Cromwell led the revolution in the British Isles within this 150-year time span. Music of the period sounds dignified, regal, repetitive and frequently complex, yet very accessible. It has a high-tech quality to it that creatures of the 20th century seem to relate to well. It is characterized by sectional contrasts: loud and soft, fast and slow, major and minor, tension and release. There is a profusion of ornamentation performed in a tasteful framework. And the great energy it exudes is always there!

Given the interest in Baroque performance practice (whereby modern-day ensembles and soloists try to reproduce, with period instruments, the music to sound as it did then), there are superb groups making recordings and concertizing to a bigger and bigger following. It is out there and it is easy to get to.

Mechanically, everything that composers had been groping for in the preceding centuries came together in the Baroque period: notation, a system of tuning, forms, rhythm and harmony. Instruments continued to improve, too. The most popular were the harpsichord, clavichord (also a keyboard), organ, a variety of strings called gambas and viols, the guitar-like mandolins and lutes, brasses and recorders (early flutes).

Vivaldi, for example, wrote some 500 concertos which highlight one or more instruments accompanied by a small orchestra. Keyboard music, written primarily for organ or harpsichord, became more virtuosic and improvisatory-sounding, with pieces called toccatas, fugues and preludes. The *sonata (an instrumental piece of contrasting large sections for one or more instruments)* was speeding toward its culmination in the late 18th century.

The big headline item in the Baroque period was the flowering of opera. Italian composers, Jacopo Peri (1561-1633) and Giulio Caccini (1550-1618), were the originators of this art form. But Claudio Monteverdi (remember him from the Renaissance?) wrote the first successful, viable opera, *Orfeo,* which was presented in 1607.

Other vocal music gained momentum during these years. Handel's *Messiah* is a superb example of an *oratorio: a large, unstaged dramatic work on a religious subject.* A staple in the *oeuvre* of J. S. Bach was *the secular counterpart* – namely, the *cantata.*

Before getting into the details about the more well-known Stock Baroquers, here are some brief profiles of other noteworthy Baroquers:

Giovanni Gabrieli (c.1555-1612)

Known for dramatic contrasts in his music. St. Mark's in Venice was his concert hall. He had choirs and instruments in different locations (i.e. balconies), playing in dizzying alternation. Penetrating brass music.

Girolamo Frescobaldi (1583-1643)

The greatest keyboard composer of his time, his style combined chromaticism, sharp dissonance, and a tension-producing unpredictable texture. Though his music sounds improvised, it is shrewdly calculated.

Heinrich Schutz (1585-1672)

German court musician at Dresden who wrote sacred vocal music of great charm.

Henry Purcell (c.1659-1695)

England's composer of all composers. Wrote goosebump brass music. Celebrated in court for his church music and odes and songs of welcome, he became well-known for his theater music. "When I am laid in earth" from Act 3 of his only full and famous opera, *Dido and Aeneas,* is a masterpiece of Baroque pathos.

And while many a bride may think she is processing down the aisle to Purcell's *Trumpet Voluntary,* also known as *The Prince of Denmark's March*, she is in fact swishing the satin to a piece written in 1700 by Jeremiah Clarke, an English composer and organist.

Jean-Baptiste Lully (1632-1687)

Louis XIV's main music man, Lully wrote twenty *tragédies lyriques* (operas), tailored to his king's tastes. He succeeded in creating a new French style of dramatic declamation, appropriate to the natural rhythms of the French language.

Jean-Philippe Rameau (1683-1764)

French opera and opera-ballet composer, in a heroic but elegant style. Brilliant theorist and philosopher.

The Violin Makers

Andrea Amati brought Italian violin-making into the fore in the mid-1500s. But the craft peaked from 1650 to 1750, with Niccolò Amati and his protégés, Giuseppe Guarneri and Antonio Stradivari, and the Austrian Jacob Stainer.

And not to be overlooked are:

Domenico Scarlatti (1685-1757)

Son of famous opera composer, Alessandro. Italian keyboard virtuoso who once got in a harpsichord duel with Handel in Rome. Wrote numerous harpsichord sonatas.

Georg Philipp Telemann (1681-1767)

A German who played many instruments and who was famous in his day. Wrote his first opera at the age of 12. Massive output in all possible forms. Known for his orchestral suites and concertos.

Arcangelo Corelli (1653-1713)

Violinist *extraordinaire*. President of the Roman musician's union. Set the seal on the concerto grosso and synthesized the budding sonata. Buried next to Raphael in the Pantheon.

Johann Pachelbel (1653-1706)

If we hear that *Canon* in D one more time...

François Couperin (1668-1733)

French composer who wrote instrumental music for Louis XIV. Massive output of harpsichord music.

Tomaso Albinoni (1671-1750)

Prolific Italian composer of expressive concertos. Beware of *Adagio* for strings; it was pieced together from three scant original fragments in 1945 by an Italian musicologist – who filled in the rest.

And now, onto the bullish Baroquers who are the principals of the musical firm, Bach, Handel, Vivaldi & Co.:

Johann Sebastian Bach (1685-1750)

With the wonder of computers came the commercialization of Bach. For a TV-watching target market, his contrapuntal capers transcribed beautifully onto a high-tech keyboard or dashboard for that matter. And that was just the beginning.

Anybody who wants their product to sound smart (ergo superior) turns to the keyboard music of Bach. Why? Because it is fingery, busy, mathematically perfect stuff. It has momentum and repetition, and at times can sound downright mechanical, even technical. Foreign automobile makers were the first to use Bach's music as background in their pedal-to-the-metal-on-the-Autobahn ads. Other music by Bach, such as one of the six *Brandenburg Concertos* and excerpts from a collection of pieces compiled by his second wife, Anna Magdalena, sells yogurt, pitches real estate and in a contemporary guise occasionally creeps into a top ten popular hit.

Undoubtedly, you have heard his music. It has been Switched-On and Jazzed-Up, and maintains its integrity no matter how it is abused.

Bach is undisputedly one of the greatest composers of all time. He brought the art of *contrapuntal writing* (a texture of more than one melody sounding simultaneously) to its peak. One could say he exhausted all the possibilities. In his day he was considered somewhat of a dinosaur. Only in the early 19th century was the genius of his music DISCOVERED, and he has been leading off the Classical music triumvirate ever since: Bach, Beethoven and Brahms (referred to as the Three Bs)

Born in Eisenach, Germany, on March 21, 1685 into a musical family that prospered for six generations, Bach led a simple, countrified life. His jobs were mostly as church organist and choir director (Lutheran), or court composer, and he wrote music according to the requirements of those posts.

But Bach was no bore. There was the scene in the street with one of his female singers. He was jailed for wanting to get out of a job. He was denied a job he won in a competition because he would not grease the judges' palms. And he was found in the organ loft with his future wife MAKING MUSIC.

He fathered twenty children (P. D. Q. Bach is not one of his biological offspring) during two marriages. His most musical children were: J. C. (Johann Christian), C. P. E. (Carl Philipp Emanuel), and W. F. (Wilhelm Friedemann).

In the end, his eyes failed badly, and a famous eye specialist performed two gruesome operations which left Bach permanently blind. In 1750 he suddenly regained his vision, but it was the case of the light-bulb burning more brightly just before it goes out. Ten days later he was dead.

Greatest Hits:

> *Air* for G String
>
> *Art of the Fugue*
>
> *Brandenburg Concertos*
>
> *Chaconne* for Unaccompanied Violin
>
> *Chromatic Fantasy & Fugue*
>
> *The Goldberg Variations*
>
> *Inventions*
>
> *Italian Concerto*
>
> *Jesu, Joy of Man's Desiring*
>
> *Mass* in B minor
>
> *Musical Offering*
>
> *Notebook for Anna Magdalena Bach*
>
> *St. John Passion*
>
> *St. Matthew Passion*

Sheep May Safely Graze

Toccata & Fugue in D minor

Well-Tempered Clavier

NOTE: Bach's music is categorized by BWV followed by a number. The initials stand for *Bach-Werke-Verzeichnis* (Catalogue of Bach's Works).

George Frideric Handel (1685-1759)

HAL-LE-LU-JAH!

You can hear the four-syllable exclamation following any incident of triumphant revelation, such as remembering where you put the car keys, achieving a conquest of the flesh, or even upon delivering a newborn baby. It erupts as easily from the mouthguard of a victorious football player as it does from the quivering lips of a jet-load of frightened passengers who have just touched down.

Handel's present-day claim to fame is that single word and its catchy musical setting. Everybody knows at least that much of the composer's *"Hallelujah"* chorus from his oratorio, *Messiah*, which he wrote in three weeks. The piece is so riveting and uplifting that to attend the Messiah Sing-In at Lincoln Center in New York is like being at a Rolling Stones concert: people are jumping up and down on the seats, screaming and yelling when it is over and demanding an encore and getting it.The tradition of standing up for the *"Hallelujah"* chorus began when King George I was overcome with emotion and rose to his feet. One seems to do it instinctively, however.

But Handel always generated excitement. He was the sophisticated traveler, the darling of the crowned heads of Europe. He got into a duel over a harpsichord part in a friend's opera. He hung around with the Medicis, and then England's Queen Anne and later King George. Handel settled in England, teaching the young royals and producing operas.

Handel's travels enabled him to synthesize styles from his native land, Germany, as well as those of France, Italy and England, making him a truly international composer. He wrote beautiful, expressive melodies and had a feel for the theater. Where Bach was a culminator, Handel was an innovator. It is a fascinating dichotomy when one realizes that both men were born the same year and just a few miles apart.

He was known as a fair-minded man, payed his bills on time and managed his money well. His sense of humor was described as "dry wit", and he could swear in many languages. His food bills reached the top of the proscenium as he was a voracious and appreciative gormandizer. His love life consisted of numerous short encounters. Like Bach, he suffered from failing eyesight.

In his seventy-fourth year he died in his London home and was buried in Westminster Abbey with 3,000 people in attendance.

Greatest Hits:

> *Acis and Galatea*
> *Arrival of the Queen of Sheba*
> *Concerti Grossi*
> *The Harmonious Blacksmith*
> *Israel in Egypt*
> *Jeptha*
> *"Largo"* from *Xerxes*
> *Messiah*
> *"Minuet"* from *Berenice*
> *Royal Fireworks Music*
> *See the Conquering Hero Comes*
> Sonatas (violin, flute, recorder)
> *Water Music*

Antonio Vivaldi (1678-1741)

Who has not heard the buoyant strains of Vivaldi's Baroque mastery selling gourmet mustard, accompanying ice dancing at the Olympics, or pushing real estate for a certain clientele?

Nicknamed Mr. Baroque in this century, and *Il prete rosso* in his own day, "the red-haired priest" wrote the feel-good light variety music that has found a huge following among today's aging Yuppies foundering in the time-warp between Fleetwood Mac and Mahler.

Listening to his music, you would never suspect that Vivaldi was an unsavory character. Needless to say, he did not last long as a man of the cloth; it seems he gave himself communion more often than anyone. And those holy togs were frequently shed for fleshy pursuits.

But this controversial man represented the progressive Italian musical thought of his time. With Venice as his home base and his father his violin teacher, Vivaldi became one of the foremost violinists in the region and had a loyal entourage and long appointments by patrons. His longest and most tumultuous association was with the Ospedale della Pieta in Venice, an institution for foundling girls with a superb choir and orchestra. He also became leading violinist at St. Mark's.

He composed around 700 instrumental works and dozens of vocal pieces and scores of operas.

But by 1740 Vivaldi fell out of favor with the Venetian public, and ended up in Vienna where he died, penniless.

Today, Vivaldi's most recognizable composition is *The Four Seasons,* instrumental music from a collection written around 1725 called *The Contest Between Harmony and Invention*. It represents the composer's first real venture into program music (music which illustrates a story). For example, in the *"Winter Concerto"*, Vivaldi masterfully portrays chilling cold, a frightening wind, chattering teeth, raindrops, a nervous ice-skater who stumbles, cracking ice and the struggle between the sirocco and the north wind. In others he depicts a drunkard, a peasant dance, a hunt and a hail storm – to name a few.

No wonder Madison Avenue loves Vivaldi.

Greatest Hits:

Concerto alla Rustica
The Four Seasons
Mandolin Concerti
Take your pick of the 500 concerti.

Test Your B. Q.

A Multiple Choice Test of Your Baroque Quotient

1. *Fugue*:
   a) an ongoing fight between the Hatfields and the McCoys.
   b) a foreign obscenity.
   c) a multi-voice piece with a theme (subject) tossed around between the parts.

2. *Well-Tempered*:
   a) having a nice disposition.
   b) a system of tuning still in use.
   c) a climate-controlled water source.

3. *Viol*:
   a) a small glass tube.
   b) something detestable.
   c) an early stringed instrument similar to the violin.

4. *Ground Bass*:
   a) a fish paté.
   b) home plate.
   c) a repeating pattern of notes in the lowest voice.

5. *"When I Am Laid..."*
   a) the anticipated rite of passage of a young man.
   b) the anticipated rite of passage of a young girl.
   c) the anticipated rite of burial of the heroine Dido in Purcell's opera, *Dido and Aeneas*, 1689.

Test Your B.Q Answers

Answers: 1. c, 2. b, 3. c, 4. c, 5. c

Movement 4

Classical Colossi:
Haydn and Mozart, then Beethoven

"Haydn, Mozart and Beethoven developed a new art, whose origins first appear in the middle of the eighteenth century."

E.T.A. Hoffmann, in 1814,
quoted in Charles Rosen, *The Classical Style* (1971)

Movement 4

Classical Colossi:
Haydn & Mozart, then Beethoven

Haydn and Mozart are constantly uttered in the same breath along the lines of salt and pepper, bread and butter, and Visa and Mastercard. Historically speaking, these alleged Classical clones of the 18th century are so inextricably tied to one another that they seem interchangeable, particularly to the general public. However, there are differences between them and their compositional styles and contributions – but within the context of the Classical Period, which roughly encompasses the years 1750 to 1825.

Try to think of Haydn and Mozart – who frequently have an ampersand placed between their names like "A & P" – as individuals in the following way:

Haydn	_Mozart_
Mercedes	Ferrari
Wine	Champagne
Brooks Brothers	Armani
Hobe Sound	St. Tropez
Le Cirque	Planet Hollywood
Bathtub	Jacuzzi

GET THE PICTURE?

Simply put, even though one's an apple and the other's an orange, they are both fruits. Mozart's a little zestier.

And what of Beethoven?   TOP BANANA.

Haydn called him "The Great Mogul". Mozart said of the young, 16-year old Beethoven, to "keep your eyes on him; some day he will give the world something to talk about." Beethoven's comment after having instruction with Haydn was, typically, "I never learned anything from him." However, upon learning of Haydn's passing, Beethoven wept.

Artistically, historically, and personally, Beethoven cannot be linked with anyone. He is a separate, brilliant entity, culminating and innovating simultaneously. His music speaks to humanity but he could not relate to people.

So, where did this precocious 16-year old end up in the context of the Classical Period? Here's a formula:

Haydn is to Mozart is to Beethoven as...

The Matterhorn is to K2 is to Mount Everest

or

Wilt Chamberlain is to Dennis Rodman is to Michael Jordan.

These are thoroughly opinionated analogies. Many consider Mozart the Everest of composers. Furthermore, Beethoven is often regarded as a Romantic composer. He straddles both periods – the Classic and the Romantic. Numerous aspects of his life are typically Romantic, but his music uses the elements of the Classical style and transcends them.

Haydn, Mozart and Beethoven all worked in and around Vienna, distilling music to its purest elements. So brilliant were they – first Haydn and his younger contemporary Mozart, and then egomaniacal upstart Beethoven – that in the historical equivalent of a blink of an eye, they developed Classical music: *the standard by which all other music is measured*. They polished the already established forms of the symphony, concerto, sonata and string quartet, and within those forms they maintained a strict aesthetic. The four-measure phrase and the eight-measure period, still crucial to successful composition and evident in everything from rap to Sondheim, became solidly entrenched once and for all.

The piano, created early in the 18th century in Italy, offered endless possibilities with its *forte* (loud) and *piano* (soft) capabilities as opposed to the less expressive sound of the harpsichord and its relatives. The earliest pianos were called the *fortepiano*, Bach supposedly owned one; but it was Mozart and Beethoven who brought the piano into the mainstream when they played concerts and wrote music specifically for it.

How does the music sound compared to that of the Baroque? Gone are the extreme and severe sectional contrasts. Classical music is a study in exquisite moderation: gradations within areas of loud and soft, pivotal cushions between major and minor, and subtle manipulation of our senses.

UNTIL BEETHOVEN!

Rules are made to be broken. Beethoven bent them into the Romantic period.

And if Mozart had lived longer, who knows? He might have ended up in a different chapter altogether.

Franz Joseph Haydn (1732-1809)

Like the air we breathe, Haydn is so prevalent he is practically invisible. Every orchestra programs a number of his 104 symphonies, every string quartet plays some of his 83 compositions for that medium, and nearly all pianists encounter one of his 47 or so keyboard sonatas. The music is elegant, non-confrontational perfection that is enjoyable to play and easy on the ear. It gently tugs at the emotions, keeps the interest and is often witty.

As innocuous as his music seems to be, Haydn employed innovative compositional techniques in harmonic expansion and rhythmic propulsion, and helped standardize the four-movement formula of the string quartet and the symphony. In string quartets, he gave equal weight to all four instruments, not just highlighting the violin with the others in accompaniment.

But talk about a late bloomer! Haydn, a former Vienna Choirboy, did not get himself propelled until he was almost thirty years old, when he penned his first symphony. Mozart tossed his first one off at age seven.

Eventually he found his way to the post of Kapellmeister at the estate of the immensely wealthy Hungarian noble family of Esterházy. During this thirty-plus year stint, he earned the nickname, Papa Haydn, because of the benevolent way he looked after the palace musicians.

By 1790 Haydn's association with the nobles had come to an end. At that time he relocated to Vienna becoming a fast friend of Mozart whom he called "the greatest composer known to me either in person or by name." Later on, he took on an obnoxious student named Beethoven.

Having already visited London with great success in 1791, he returned there in 1794 and wrote his twelve *London* symphonies as well as his oratorio, *The Creation*. About a decade later he died in his sleep.

Haydn's symphonies reflect his witty genius at work. The *Clock Symphony* contains a ticking sound produced by the orchestra. Of the surprise in his *Surprise Symphony*, a sudden loud chord, Haydn himself said, "That will make the ladies scream." The *Farewell* was composed to drop a hint to Prince Nikolaus Esterházy that his musicians were restless about visiting their families and that he should not disband the orchestra because of it. Haydn made his point rather cleverly: at the end of the symphony, one by one the musicians snuff out their candles, get up and walk off stage.

IT WORKED.

Greatest Hits:

> *Andante con variazione* in F minor
> *The Creation*
> *Cello Concerto* in D major
> *Emperor String Quartet*
> *Keyboard Concerto* in D major
> *London* Symphonies
> *Lord Nelson Mass*
> *Paris* Symphonies
> *The Seasons*
> *Mass in Time of War*
> *Trumpet Concerto* in E-flat

Wolfgang Amadeus Mozart (1756-1791)

Leave it to a clever playwright to make a million out of a molehill. Peter Shaffer's play (and subsequent movie called *Amadeus*) exaggerated a rumor, a myth – undocumented heresay – about rival composer, Antonio Salieri, (one of Beethoven's preferred teachers) "poisoning" the young genius, Mozart. And of course, we all ate it up.

The positive outcome of *Amadeus* is that it brought Mozart's exquisite music into contact with the movie-going public. Neville Marriner and the Academy of St. Martin-in-the-Fields became a household mouthful and a must-have CD acquisition. And even several years after the movie, the third movement from the *Twenty-Second Piano Concerto* – used as background while Mozart led an outdoor concert from the piano bench – reflects the task, in all its elegant simplicity, of making pre-measured Maxwell House coffee.

And there are others, more readily recognizable familiarities not present in the movie's soundtrack: the adorable tot tune "Twinkle, Twinkle Little Star" is actually from a popular folk tune called *"Ah, Vous Dirai-je, Maman"* upon which Mozart wrote 12 charming variations; a remnant of Music Appreciation 101 might be "It's a bird, it's a plane, it's a Mozart," used to trigger the memory of the *Fortieth Symphony*; the *"Minuet"* from *Don Giovanni* epitomizes 18th century gentility; sections of *Eine Kleine*

WOLFGANG AMADEUS MOZART

Sammlungen der Gesellschaft der Musikfreunde

Nachtmusik sell everything aspiring to elegance on TV and radio; and for those who remember the film, *Elvira Madigan*, the theme comes from the slow movement of the *Concerto for Piano* in C Major, No. 21, K. 467. And if there ever was music that epitomized Mom, apple pie and home sweet home, it's the opening theme from Mozart's *Sonata* in C Major, K. 545.

Mozart's compositions are classified by the letter "K" followed by a number. This is after the chronological list first made by Ludwig von Köchel in 1862.

The ultimate child prodigy, young Mozart was dragged around Europe by his father, Leopold, and together with his sister, Nannerl, performed for the crowned heads and *haute société*. Like a sponge, Wolfgang absorbed musical styles from England, France, Italy, Austria and Germany, and this formed into his unique musical language.

At the age of twelve, he wrote two operas, one of which received a private performance thanks to the persuasive powers of Dr. Anton Mesmer, the man who invented hypnotism. A few years and lost jobs later, Mozart married his equal in immaturity and irresponsibility, Constanze. They had six children, two survived. Without a formal appointment, Mozart earned money by teaching and filling commissions. In 1784 Mozart and Haydn became Freemasons and friends.

After women, it was opera that Mozart lusted for, and he proved his genius in this genre. He came into contact with the librettist, Lorenzo Da Ponte, the result being *The Marriage of Figaro*, *Don Giovanni* and *Cosi Fan Tutti*. Interestingly, Da Ponte emigrated to America, selling groceries in Pennsylvania and ultimately becoming the first professor of Italian at Columbia University. A collaboration with fellow Freemason Emanuel Schikaneder led to *The Magic Flute* which met with success.

But Mozart's health and finances were in a downward spiral. In November of 1791 he worked on his *Requiem* from bed, and a month later at age thirty-five, went to sleep and never woke up. No one knows where the body is or the cause of death. Some medical sleuthing points to kidney disease, but no one is truly certain.

Greatest Hits:

> *Clarinet Concerto*
> *Eine Kleine Nachtmusik*
> Operas:
> *The Abduction From the Seraglio*
> *Cosi Fan Tutte*

Don Giovanni
The Magic Flute
The Marriage of Figaro
Symphonies:
    Nos. 29, 38 *(Prague),* 39, 40, 41 *(Jupiter)*
Piano Concertos: Nos. 20-27
Overtures
String Quartets

Ludwig van Beethoven (1770-1827)

Beethoven has been called the personification of music.Beethoven has been called the Atlas of the musical world. And Beethoven has been called its tragic hero.

In the hearts of many musicians and composers, it is Beethoven they must answer to. His music fills the seats in the concert halls; people connect with him and feel his message. Universally, Beethoven is acknowledged as one of the greatest composers of all time.

His music permeates our lives. The four opening notes in that riveting rhythm from his *Fifth Symphony* parallel the Morse Code of three dots and a dash (the letter V), which signalled victory to the Allied troops during World War II. There may be people who are ignorant of who inked those four notes, but they sure can sing them. People will utter "Tah-Tah-Tah Tuhhhhh" whenever there is a dramatic turn of events, and inherent in those few notes, is an unsettling ambiguity: is the event threatening or beneficial; serious or amusing? Head-turning, to be sure.

After the *Fifth Symphony*, most of us have sung or heard the melody from the final movement of his *Ninth Symphony*, also known as the *"Ode to Joy"*. When the New York Rangers raised their Stanley Cup Banner in Madison Square Garden, it was this music of Beethoven's, accompanied by a thrilling laser display, that electrified the fans. So powerful is this achievement of his final symphony, that since Beethoven's death a "curse" has loomed among other composers who cannot seem to crank out more than nine symphonies. Some of those include Schubert, Bruckner, Dvořák, Mahler and Vaughan Williams.

Yes, he was an untamed man. Yes, he went on sojourns of madness, disappearing in the woods for days. And yes, his appearance was unruly. So what. He was the first composer to be treated like royalty BY royalty, instead of as a servant. He overcame a childhood fraught with abuse from an alcoholic father. He was orphaned by the age of 22 but had been supporting his parents and two brothers from a much younger age. And yes, he went deaf at an early age – around 29.

But he could hear in his head, and he could hear on paper. Imagine being able to hear all the instruments of an orchestra playing the finished product in your head. Beethoven composed some of his greatest masterpieces while he was deaf. And composing was not easy for him; he sketched and sketched, revised and rewrote. Mozart, on the other hand, had it all figured out in his head and made one copy of what he composed.

Virginia Bates

LUDWIG VAN BEETHOVEN

Technically, Beethoven pushed the set forms of the Classical period to new limits. His musical language was daring in its day. You can hear the dramatic, almost schizophrenic differences within the music; the serene and the stormy. His sudden shifts in rhythm heighten the drama.

Beethoven's last years saw the famous violent outbursts, the irascible behavior, the sudden rages. You can feel the frustration. According to legend, on the afternoon of March 26, 1827 a raging thunderstorm broke out. Beethoven lay upon his deathbed. There was a great flash of lightning, and Beethoven opened his eyes and shook his fist angrily at the sky. "I shall hear in Heaven!" he proclaimed, then sank back into bed and died. But, in fact, Beethoven was too weak from fever even to raise his arm.

Over 10,000 people gathered for the funeral procession in Vienna. He is buried in Vienna's Central Cemetery, along with Franz Schubert.

Greatest Hits:

> *Archduke Piano Trio*
> *"Für Elise",* Bagatelle for Piano
> *Coriolan Overture*
> *Diabelli Variations* for Piano
> *Egmont Overture*
> *Fidelio (*opera*)*
> *Leonore Overture* No. 3
> *Minuet in G* for Piano

Piano Concertos:
> Nos. 1 - 5

Piano Sonatas:
> *Appassionata*
> *Moonlight*
> *Pathétique*
> *Waldstein*

Rasumovsky String Quartets
Septet, Op. 20
Symphonies:
> Nos. 3 *(Eroica),* 5, 6 *(Pastoral),* 7 and
> 9 *(Choral)*
> *"Turkish March"* from *The Ruins of Athens*
> *Violin Concerto* in D major

Violin Sonatas:
> *Kreutzer*
> *The Spring*

Missa Solemnis

The Late String Quartets

Classical Cohorts

Haydn, Mozart and Beethoven were not the only composers working and thriving in the 18th and 19th centuries. Here are year-book type snippets of the Colossi's cohorts.

Carl Philipp Emanuel Bach (1714-1788)

Fifth son of J. S. ... profoundly influenced Haydn and Mozart ... photographic memory...more popular than his dad ... known for the emotionalism in his music, *"Empfindsamer Stile"*.

> *Best Buys:*
>> Symphonies
>> Flute Sonatas

Johann Christian Bach (1735-1782)

Last son of J. S. – a passion for Italian opera – lived in London and met the eight-year old Mozart there and influenced him as a composer, preferred the new piano and helped it into the limelight. A.k.a. the London Bach.

> *Best Buys:*
>> Quintets
>> *Concerto for Bassoon* in B-flat
>> Symphonies

Luigi Boccherini (1743-1805)

Italian cellist *extraordinaire*, a member of the first professional traveling string quartet, invented the string quintet.

Best Buys:
> Guitar Quintets
> Cello Concertos

Luigi Cherubini (1760-1842)

An Italian in Paris, opera composer. His opera, *Médéé*, influenced Beethoven.

Best Buys:
> *Médéé* (Medea)
> *Requiem* in D Minor

Muzio Clementi (1752-1832)

Famous pianist and teacher revered in his own time (what piano student has not played those harder-than-they-look sonatinas), greatly influenced Beethoven, became a piano manufacturer and publisher, heard Franz Liszt and threw in the musical towel.

Best Buys:
> Sonatas
> Sonatinas

Christoph Willibald Gluck (1714-1787)

A pivotal figure in opera history. His monumental opera, *Orfeo ed Euridice*, had continuous music that reflected mood and action.

Best Buys:
> *Orfeo*
> *Don Juan* (Ballet)

Johann Nepomuk Hummel (1778-1837)

Piano prodigy, charmed Mozart into teaching him, obese and unkempt, succeeded Haydn at Esterháza, the castle of the Esterházys.

Best Buys:

> Chamber Music
> Piano Works
> Two Piano Concertos
> Trumpet Concerto

Antonio Salieri (1750-1825)

Did NOT poison Mozart (DID look out for himself at the court), opera a specialty, taught Beethoven, Schubert, Liszt, Hummel and Czerny, went bonkers in the end (claiming "I killed Mozart!"), makes for great copy – right, Mr. Shaffer?

Best Buys:

> Piano Concertos
> Opera Overtures

Giovanni Battista Sammartini (1700-1775)

Extended three movement sinfonie to Classical model of four movements (68 symphonies).

Best Buys:

> There are hardly any recordings. If you can
> find them, buy them.

Johann Wenzel Anton Stamitz (1717-1757)

Bohemian violinist and conductor who put together the prototype of the modern symphony orchestra in Mannheim, Germany. The ensemble became famous for its precision in dynamics (soft to louds and back). He developed the first really virtuoso orchestra.

Best Buys:

> Symphonies
> Flute Concertos
> Clarinet Concerto

Movement 5

Romantic Antics

"...That infinite longing which is the essence of Romanticism."

E. T. A. Hoffman, in 1813,
quoted in Headington,
The Bodley Head History of Western Music (1974)

"All that doodle, doodle."

Rudolf Serkin,
quoted in Jacobson,
Reverberations (1975)

Movement 5

Romantic Antics

If you ever forget what the big buzzword of 19th century Romantic music is, think of it this way:

RoMANtic music

"MAN"

(Feminists, relax. The author uses this term as a derivative of "huMANity".)

A period in music history which practically defies definition, the Romantic era, it is generally held, is demarcated by Beethoven's death in1827 and a "tonality-shattering" composition by Arnold Schoenberg in 1911.

The big news of the 19th century was that the compositional focus shifted from the cool, detached, controlled sophistication of Classicism, to MAN and how he relates to everything, and vice versa. Here are but a few examples:

MAN and Nature
MAN and Woman

MAN and Man

MAN and Politics

MAN and God

MAN and Satan

MAN and Music

MAN and His Audience

MAN and His Instruments.

And of all the periods in music history, the Romantic era produced the most singable melodies, whether from opera or piano concertos. Many Romantic themes have been reincarnated into popular hits, such as *"Could It Be Magic"*, Barry Manilow's spin on Chopin's brooding *"Prelude"; or "Tonight We Love"*, taken from Tchaikovsky's *Piano Concerto No. 1*. Cartoons were catapulted into mainstream popularity when Romantic music reflected the animated action. From Bugs Bunny's spoofing Wagner in *"What's Opera, Doc?"* to The Ren and Stimpy Show's outrageous take on *"Anitra's Dance"* from Grieg's *Peer Gynt Suite* No. 1, this collaboration signaled a new way to bring Romantic music into every plugged-in household.

As for television and radio commercials, let us just say Romantic composers unknowingly wrote more jingles than are found on Santa's sleigh. Romantic music is enjoying a renaissance in the 1990s, whether lifted literally or in some inspired, time-tapered version. The trend gains momentum around the holidays with Chopin helping seduce the perfume buyer. From there it goes on to fine wrist-watch pitches. Where in the 1980's it was Bach and Vivaldi pushing cars and computers, now it is Puccini's *Madama Butterfly* setting hearts aflutter for an automobile. Or it is Schumann's warm-and-fuzzy (and slightly re-interpreted) *Scenes From Childhood* for baby formula. In another spot, a soprano (once again) sets up the viewer for a hilarious ad that begins with a romantically-inclined couple crossing a room toward one another – until he trips and brings down a whole Babette's feast onto the carpet –

a luxurious yet stain-resistant carpet. Pop star, Aaron Neville, croons soothingly with a soulful Brahms' *"Lullaby"* while a businessman crosses the ocean in cozy nighttime aero-comfort (just like home) on Delta Airlines. Romantic music and cocooning seem a match made in heaven.

What makes this media-music marriage so effective is Romantic music's inherent *EMOTION*. Romantic era composers went all out to project and manipulate emotions. They strove for reactions, even reactions to how they were reacting. They accomplished this in at least two ways:

First, they played with musical language, toying with the very vocabulary of traditional harmony. Where Mozart would venture not too far from a home-base key such as F major by going to its close relative D minor, Mahler, starting in the same place, would travel far afield – pivoting his way around tonality to its apogee until an eventual (and to the listener's relief) triumphant return to his home base. With Mozart it is a visit to a next-door neighbor, with Mahler, a whirlwind global tour. Add to this formula expanded use of rhythm. While metronomic beat-keeping still persisted if it suited the compositional goal, Romantic composers achieved drama through strategically-placed pauses, sudden and extreme shifts in tempo, and elasticized phrasing (rubato). It is sometimes difficult to tap your foot steadily all the way through a Romantic piece.

Second, Romantic era composers were aided and abetted by the improved technological capabilities of instruments. There were wider compasses (ranges) and therefore more notes; from the very low to the very high. Instruments were able to be played very loudly or very softly; very quickly or very slowly. Those doing the performing rose to the challenge of the refined instruments. This was the age of the *VIRTUOSO* player. The most famous virtuosi were the demonic violinist, Paganini, and the equally maniacal pianist, Liszt, – the true heavy-metal patriarch.

And they were the first to break their instruments on stage. Take note, Pete Townsend.

NOTE: Pete Townsend, of The Who, was one of the first modern rock stars to smash his guitar in concert. Many others followed.

To further their artistic cause, composers tinkered with the forms established in the Classical period. One example: Think of the symphonic form as a balloon. In the Classical period it was nicely inflated and knotted at the end. By the waning years of the 19th century, however, that symphonic balloon was blown to its absolute latex limits, just a breath away from exploding. (Guess what happens in the 20th century?) At the other end of the formal spectrum (in this period there is always The Other End), are the character pieces and salon pieces. These are short, musical sketches: some are difficult while others are not, most are symmetrical in form and are written for an intimate venue. They go by such names as *nocturne*, *bagatelle*, *étude* and *intermezzo*, to list a few. And they are usually written for the piano.

The German *LIED* (pronounced LEED) or art song became a major *tour de force* thanks to Franz Schubert.

> *The Lied is a composition for solo voice with piano accompaniment, based on a German poem. The "art" is in the synergy between the text and the music.*

PROGRAM MUSIC, which was wholly instrumental, *told a story, reflected emotions, or described an event pictorially in music.*

ABSOLUTE MUSIC was the opposite: *it had NO extra-musical connotations, just the composer's inspiration and craft.*

And in the 19th century, opera reached its apex, its Golden Age. Set in motion by Monteverdi in the Baroque era and Mozart in the Classical period, composers like Rossini, Donizetti and Weber revolutionized opera and opened up the artistic possibilities for those to follow, namely: Wagner, Verdi, Puccini and Strauss. When people think of opera, this is IT. At the hands of these composers, opera truly became "music drama," wherein the music actually took on the life of the opera's characters.

Composers in the Romantic period manipulated all musical parameters to be as literal as ever; whether in simulating the whirring of a spinning wheel, a macabre opium-induced march to the scaffold, a train of thought or an impulse. It was all about *EXPRESSION*.

Someone once said it is better to generate controversy than indifference. Romantic period composers – some deliberately and others unknowingly – seemed to live by this tenet. And they all had impassioned opinions about music, whether it was theirs or someone else's. Some worked quite hard to make those opinions known, too: drawing battle lines, splintering off into various factions, engaging in manifesto wars, or in smear campaigns, character defamation, posturing, caustic criticisms, backbiting and back-stabbing. Having a strong viewpoint was about the only common bond between these highly individualistic compositional characters.

It was all very much a reflection of the political situation in Western Europe. While real soldiers fought real wars both in Europe and in America, philosophical wars raged amongst the Romantics. On a grand scale, you had Wagnerians on one side and anti-Wagnerians on the other. On a microcosmic level, you had warring factions within one person, such as in Robert Schumann and his multiple personalities. More movies have been made about the tortured lives of Romantic composers, like Beethoven, Schumann, Chopin and Liszt, than about any others.

The Romantic poet, Goethe said in 1827, "Classicism is health, romanticism is sickness."

This chapter might well have been called "The Manic Romantics."

Despite all this torment and torture, the body of work emanating from this period is the staple of programming both in concert halls and opera houses. It is beautiful and ugly, difficult and easy, complex and naive, accessible and bewildering. Some of the music carries a message. It is fantasy, it is reality.

Even today, 19th century music brings out the best and worst in people. Some love its poignancy, others call it sappy. Some revel in its sheer muscle, others find it oppressive. Some find it profound, Rudolph Serkin called it "doodle-doodle." Some are caught up in its yearning, others pine for its last notes. It is probably the most talked-about period in music. It is certainly the most listened-to and performed.

Because Romantic music encompasses a vast period, not only in duration but in creative scope, it is presented here in four sections:

Romantic "Characters"

Romantic "Opera-tors"

The Late Heavies

Neo, Geo, and Where Do We Go From Here?

Romantic "Characters"

A character piece is, by definition, a composition usually for the piano, which expresses a programmatic idea or a single mood. Led off by none other than Beethoven, there is an unprecedented amount of moodiness among composers in the 19th century! (Robert Schumann had several going at once.) This phenomenon dovetails nicely with the form.

Here then, are the most important Romantic "Characters" – presented in pieces.

Franz Schubert (1797-1828)

Oh, how Schubert suffered!

In his brief, lonely, 31-year existence, he was said to have been happy about three weeks.

He was so short (4' 11") that the army rejected him, and so near-sighted that the oval-framed metal spectacles never left his face.

A steady job eluded him, as did a steady love-interest. It has been said that resultant one-night stands led to his contracting what is believed to have been syphilis, which caused his chronic health problems and may have accelerated his untimely death. However, there is no evidence to substantiate this.

Schubert eventually became a pupil of Salieri (Yes, THAT Salieri) and got out from under his father's wishes to teach basic academics at the family school. He lived only to compose. At night there were those famous Schubertiads – intimate musical evenings with his friends followed by the composer having to be poured into his bed.

But his music never betrayed his misery. Through all his suffering, at the age of seventeen Schubert brought the German *Lied* or "art song" to perfection with his *Gretchen am Spinnrade*, based on a poem by Goethe. Music and poetry became one impulse in this lyrical, poignant song. He went on to write six-hundred more *Lieder* (plural of *Lied*). Among them, the ominous, galloping *Erlkönig* (written when he was eighteen) the text of which was by the king of doom and gloom, Goethe. The hard-driving, rhythmic piano part has been lifted countless times to reflect evil in pursuit in film and on television.

In contrast, the *"Trout" Quintet* is light and amusing. Its quivering, tense string playing replicates the movements of that tricky sport fish, and the bright upper-register arpeggiated octaves of the piano shimmer like a cold coursing stream. The *"Trout" Quintet* takes its name from Schubert's own song, *Die Forelle*, upon which he wrote a set of variations for the quintet's fourth movement.

His symphonies did not catch the public fancy until late in his life, and the majority were not performed until after his death. The *Unfinished Symphony*, only two movements long, is well-known for its inspired cello theme. In total there were nine magnificent symphonies, and ideas for a half-dozen more.

Dizzy spells, stomach problems, and finally delirium were the last recorded symptoms of the composer. He was buried near Beethoven, whom he raved about on his deathbed, and sixty years later the two were moved to Vienna's Central Cemetery, with Brahms nearby. The First Viennese Triumvirate was complete.

Greatest Hits:

> *NOTE*: Schubert's works are classified by "D." numbers, after the thematic catalogue of scholar Otto Eric Deutsch. Example: *Piano Sonata* in A major, D. 664.

> Symphonies:
>> Nos. 5, 8, 9

> Songs and Song Cycles:
>> *Gretchen am Spinnrade (*Gretchen at the Spinning Wheel*)*
>> *Die Winterreise*
>> *Erlkönig*
>> *Die schöne Müllerin*

> Chamber Music:
>> *"Trout" Quintet*
>> *String Quartet* for two cellos
>> Piano Trios
>> *Wind Octet*
>> String Quartets: A minor, D minor
>> *Death and the Maiden*
>> *Quartetsatz*

Piano Music:

    Six *"Moments musicaux"*

    Three *"Klavierstucke"*

    Wanderer Fantasy

    Four *"Impromptus"*

Carl Maria von Weber (1786-1826)

Not exactly a household name, Weber should be remembered as the first Romantic composer of German opera.

It is hard to imagine what direction German opera would have taken without Weber. In his great work, *Der Freischütz*, European Romanticism and German operatic traditions came together, changing the course of music history. Weber fused German nationalistic elements, such as folk songs, myths and legends with his own idiomatic style. He went for effect. The finale of Act II has been labeled "An Arsenal of Romanticism". The entire opera contains references to everything from nationalism to nature worship, the supernatural to the suggestive. You can feel the magic bullets hit their mark, thanks to the slowly plucked bass strings. And there is nothing more chilling than the Wolf's Glen scene with its howling evil spirits.

Weber was born into a musical family, his father being music director of a traveling theatrical troupe, and uncle to Mozart's singing wife, Constanze. Setting the stage for a lifetime of ills, Weber was born frail and crippled in one hip because his mother had tuberculosis during the pregnancy. The youngster traveled with the Weber Opera Company, and by the age of 11, was getting his compositions published.

As an adult, Weber always owed money, was once arrested and jailed for treason and theft, fell in love numerous times, and started to have chest troubles (Violins, HERE.) But his stint behind bars whipped him into maturity. He concertized as a virtuoso pianist and distinguished himself as a conductor. While he composed in a variety of genres, it was operas, concert music and piano compositions that earned him a place in this chapter. He settled down in 1818, marrying and having three children. In 1821 *Der Freischütz* won him popular acclaim. Shortly thereafter, he suffered his first pulmonary hemorrhage, but continued to compose. The results were *Euryanthe* and *Oberon*. The latter two operas were innovative because they were sung throughout, unlike *Der Freischütz* which had spoken dialogue.

Spitting blood and feverish, Weber nevertheless went on the road to ensure his family's financial well-being. He died in London and is buried in the Catholic Cemetery in Dresden.

Greatest Hits:

> Operas:
>> *Der Freischütz* (The Freeshooter)
>> *Euryanthe*
>> *Oberon*
>
> Concertos:
>> Two Piano Concertos
>> Two Clarinet Concertos
>> *Concertino for Clarinet and Orchestra*
>> *Concerto and Rondo for Bassoon and Orchestra*
>> *Concertino for Horn and Orchestra*
>
> Two Symphonies

Felix Mendelssohn (1809-1847)

How Mendelssohn suffers!

Suffers, as in Present Tense?

Yes – from being under-rated, under-played, under-appreciated and under-programmed.

His music has not even been formally catalogued.

In his lifetime, however, Mendelssohn had it all: money, position, personality, handsome looks, pianistic virtuosity, influence, education, the patronage of a queen, a trophy wife and five children.

He has been nicknamed The Romantic Classicist because of his brilliant symmetry of form combined with a variety of highly subjective, Romantic sentiments. The great cellist, Pablo Casals, said he was "A romantic who felt at ease within the mould of classicism." And yet, he is in a bit of a slump these days. But his time will come again. Not only did he write some wonderfully vivid music, but he championed the nearly-obscure J. S. Bach and he was a great conductor.

Mendelssohn's music is practically a sonic biography. His European travels are mapped out in his lyric symphonies and overtures: *The Hebrides* overture, the *Symphony* No. 3 (*Scottish*), and the *Symphony* No. 4 (*Italian*), all with their deeply felt nature experience. As children, he and his siblings put on Shakespeare plays, leading to his incidental music for *A Midsummer Night's Dream*, the remarkable overture which was written when he was only seventeen. His Protestantism manifests itself in a number of works, such as the great *Elijah* oratorio, the *Symphony* No. 5 (*Reformation*) and, on a lesser scale, the *Prelude and Fugue* in E minor for piano. The Bach enthusiast shows up in his organ sonatas and his *St. Paul* oratorio, to name a few examples.

Mendelssohn's ability to project a setting has won the hearts of creative directors in 20th century advertising agencies – and the public in general. The energetic *Symphony* No. 4 *(Italian)* frequently backs pasta or pizza ads – bringing an air of authenticity to the product. For a spooky setting, *The Hebrides* is almost unrivaled. And for the complete nuptial experience, his recessional staple – the *"Wedding March"* from *A Midsummer Night's Dream* gets the happy couple down the aisle and out the door.

Sometimes you will see his name appear as Mendelssohn-Bartholdy. Felix's grandfather was a German Jew named Mendelssohn. His uncle, who was a career diplomat, found his Jewishness troubling and converted to Protestantism, becoming Bartholdy after a Berlin estate he had bought. When Felix and his three siblings were baptized as Lutherans, their uncle urged them to change their name to Bartholdy. Instead, Felix's parents opted to add it.

But Mendelssohn's luck may be changing. In the 1990s, a third piano concerto was "discovered" in Oxford's Bodleian Library (England) by Mendelssohn scholar, Larry Todd. Orchestras and concert pianists all over the world have climbed all over each other for the right to premiere the piece. Time will tell if it is genuine.

The only blemish, on an otherwise perfect and brilliant career, came in 1832 when he was denied the post of his deceased teacher, Zelter, at the Singakademie – largely because of his Jewish ancestry.

Mendelssohn's fast-track life of conducting and concertizing and composing and traveling took its toll. By the fall of 1847 it was clear he was unwell. An attack (probably cardiac) of some kind put him in bed, and a week later he was dead at the age of 38.

Greatest Hits:

Music for Shakespeare's
A Midsummer Night's Dream
The Hebrides, also known as
Fingal's Cave Concert Overture

Symphonies:
No. 3 *(Scottish)*
No. 4 *(Italian)*
No. 5 *(Reformation)*

Concerto for Violin and Orchestra in E minor

Octet for Strings

Piano:
Songs Without Words (8 books)
Album Leaf in E minor
Rondo capriccioso in E minor

Oratorio:
Elijah
St. Paul

Robert Schumann (1810-1856)

Robert Schumann always traveled in a group: he and his three personalities.

It was a three-way wrestling match that lasted a lifetime. To say his music is "subjective" is an understatement – it is couch analysis. Where Weber was interested in creating a spooky effect and Mendelssohn capturing the flavor of Italy – environmental phenomena – Schumann's personalities took over the music.

He even had names for them. Florestan was the immature, capricious and tempestuous figure. Eusebius was the Bambi-eyed dreamer. And Master Raro was the judge and arbiter. It has been suggested that Florestan and Eusebius represent the manic and depressive aspects of Schumann's mental illness, with Master Raro acting as super ego. Sometimes the composer left the initials of the "author" or "authors" of a piece of music at the end.

These personalities comprised part of the *Davidsbundler*, a secret group against anything Philistine. His beloved wife, Clara Wieck, was the idolized female member of the society.

The story of Robert and Clara is the stuff of Hollywood movies (actually, there is one): he the brilliant composer/pianist and tortured soul; she, the equally talented piano virtuosa, and mother of his eight children. Because of his marriage to Clara in 1840, Schumann had one of his most prolific years as a composer. It became the year of the *Lied*, the great song cycles, including: *Dichterliebe* and *Frauenliebe und Leben*.

The piano became an extension of Schumann's personalities. In this the Romantic spirit was epitomized; being highly subjective, psychological, with music serving the emotions. He was most comfortable with the small "character" pieces for piano, often referred to as "atmospheric portraits" and "delightful pictures." In the larger forms, such as the *Piano Concerto* in A minor – possibly THE most romantic piece ever written – the piano dominates as never before, being gently buoyed by the orchestra.

Two years later the composer suffered his first breakdown. He had to quit his post as the influential editor of the *Neue Leipziger Zeitschrift für Musik* in which he and his friends led the Romantic movement. Ten rough years followed until 1852 when he had another breakdown. Yet he continued composing. Two years later his condition was so bad that he heard choirs of angels alternating with a fiendish cacophony which drove him on a stormy morning to hurl himself off the Rhine bridge. He was saved by a fisherman, and Clara subsequently had him institutionalized outside of Bonn where he died in his sleep two years later.

Greatest Hits:

Symphonies:
Symphony No. 1 in B-flat major (*Spring*)
Symphony No. 3 in E-flat major (*Rhenish*)
Symphony No. 4 (really No. 1 but that is another story)

Concerto for Piano and Orchestra in A Minor
Concerto for Cello and Orchestra in A Minor

Song Cycles:
Dichterliebe (Poet's Love)
Frauenliebe und Leben (Love and Life of Woman)

Piano:
Carnaval
Papillons
Kinderszenen
Noveletten
Albumblatter
Kreisleriana
Davidsbundlertänze (David's League)
Sonatas in F-Sharp minor, G minor and F minor
Phantasiestücke

Hector Berlioz (1803-1869)

Berlioz, the brilliant misfit.

His music was so original and controversial, that when it received performances, they were often riotous affairs; either audiences were enraptured or enraged – usually the latter. He was always broke, in trouble with his father for not living up to his expectations and made a mess of his love life, which was highly publicized. His father, a medical doctor and intellectual man, had planned for his son to follow in his footsteps. Young Berlioz did in fact study medicine in Paris for a while, but preferred cadences to cadavers. As luck would have it, the school closed, Berlioz was gaining some recognition for his compositions, and won entry into the conservatory to study music seriously. On his fourth attempt, he won the prestigious *Prix de Rome*, France's highest honor for musical composition.

He supported himself by writing music criticism, and aligned himself with the followers of the French opera composer of the Classical period, Gluck. An all-out manifesto war erupted between him and Schumann, Mendelssohn, Rossini and Wagner, to name a few of his entanglements.

One almost wonders, if he had not had such a tumultuous life, would his output of music have been so extraordinary? His innovative *Symphonie fantastique*, written in 1831 when he was 28 years old, was spawned by an obsession with a Shakespearean actress whom he eventually married (a union he later regretted). It is the fantasy of an opium-drugged artist (himself), and has an explicitly detailed program with titles such as: *"A Ball"*, *"March to the Scaffold"*, and *"Dream of a Witches' Sabbath"*. A major innovation – a recurring theme called the *idée fixe,* represents his beloved and unites the five movements.

As an orchestrator, Berlioz made ingenious use of instrumental combinations in the orchestra to vividly portray his program. Shivers run up your spine as you "hear" a guillotine drop, and then the head rolls into the basket. Of course in his day, these colorful effects earned him such designations as vulgar, without talent, a freak, charlatan, madman and a monster. Indeed, Berlioz wrote the book on orchestration, and became a conductor, the first to advocate sectional rehearsals.

A happy sojourn in Italy led to the 1834 program symphony-cum-major-viola-part, called *Harold in Italy*. It was originally requested by Paganini, who had acquired a new Stradivarius viola.

Of his operas, *Les Troyens,* is a staple in any respectable opera company's repertory. In the spring of 1990 it was selected as the debut production for the new Bastille Opera outside of Paris.

Suicide attempts, female disguises and pistol play, manifesto wars, two awful wives, enemies at every turn, the death of his son – it is amazing the man could get up in the morning. He ended up as a music librarian, having always been denied a professorship at the Paris Conservatoire. By 1865 he had completed his autobiography called *Memoires*, and his health degenerated steadily over the next four years. It is said that the horses drawing the hearse bolted for some unknown reason, and headed straight for the cemetery.

Greatest Hits:

> Symphonic Works:
>> *Symphonie fantastique*
>> *Harold in Italy*
>> Various Concert Overtures
>
> Operas:
>> *Les Troyens*
>> *Benvenuto Cellini*
>> *Beatrice et Benedict*
>> *La Damnation de Faust* (a concert opera)
>> *Romeo and Juliet* (a concert opera)
>
> Choral Music:
>> *Requiem*
>> *Te Deum*
>> *L'Enfance du Christ*

Frideric Chopin (1810-1849)

Chopin was dying all his life.

But as he suffered from increasingly degenerative bouts of tuberculosis, he ensured the immortality of the piano.

Chopin composed almost exclusively for the instrument, which, at the time of his birth, had been around for a hundred years and was becoming the new household status symbol. He understood the piano and its possibilities as no other composer, for he himself was an unsurpassed virtuoso at the keyboard. He gave the instrument a unique voice of its own. His music is an unprecedented spectrum of pianistic colors, achieved partly from exploiting the full compass, the sustaining pedal, and the dynamic possibilities of the instrument.

His melodies drew on the Italian operatic tradition, his national pride was manifested in his use of Polish dance forms, he altered Classical forms, and loaded his music with dazzling embellishments and cadenza-like passages.

In 1831, Schumann wrote about him: "Hats off gentlemen! A genius!"

A number of Chopin's works are known to almost everyone. What aspiring ballerina has not whirled her way through one of his dizzying waltzes? French perfume ads are enhanced by one of his hauntingly sensuous ballades. His *Funeral March Sonata* is the last word in that genre - the sonic equivalent of Death itself. For those of you who are thinking, well, what about that cute, spritely little 60-second *"Minute"* waltz? It is actually "my-NOOT" as in tiny. And the list of hits goes on.

Chopin was born in Poland, his father being French. Chopin integrated Polish dance forms, such as the mazurka, polonaise and waltz, into his stunningly difficult, Romantic melancholic musical vocabulary.

He led one of the most romantic lives of the Romantic composers; that is, of the *Agony and Ecstasy* variety. Coughing his way through his brief 39 years, he left Poland for good at the age of 20 and immediately became the darling of the Parisian aristocracy and later *haute société* in England and Scotland. He was refined, a G. Q. kind of dresser, and a consummate gentleman. He supported himself by teaching and giving concerts. He preferred the salon setting, and rubbed elbows with the *crème de la crème* of the art and literary worlds.

His fast-lane life-style led him to the lair of Madame Aurore Dudevant, a.k.a. George Sand, the cigar-smoking novelist whom he initially did not like. Two years later, George and Fred were an item. It lasted nine years, a period which marked Chopin's greatest creative output.

So wracked by his disease that he could no longer climb stairs, nor could he concertize, teach or compose, Chopin took to his bed in the fall of 1849. His room was crowded with visitors; loyal friends and students, curious onlookers, and numerous fainting women. He succumbed. His body was interred in the Père Lachaise cemetery in Paris. For those who visit Poland, his heart is in the Church of the Holy Cross, Warsaw.

Greatest Hits:

> *Polonaises*
> *Mazurkas*
> *Études*
> *Nocturnes*
> *Polonaise-fantaisie* in A-flat major
> *Fantaisie-impromptu* in C-sharp minor
> *Ballades*
> *Piano Concerto* No. 2 in F minor
> *Funeral March Sonata* in C minor

Franz Liszt (1811-1886)

Franz Liszt was the original Rock Star.

Clara Schumann called him "a smasher of pianos."

"His hair was so long and he had such a wild appearance," described Willert Beale.

Liszt tossed that mane of too-long hair as he unabashedly flaunted his pianistic pyrotechnics for the girls. It was no secret that the handsome Hungarian had an insatiable sexual appetite. He was said to have collected princesses and countesses as other men collect butterflies or Japanese prints or first editions. His animal magnetism made his concerts an exciting experience for throngs of women all over Europe (and probably a few men, too.)

During the Lisztomania years (1840s), the pianist took theatrics to new heights – all with very sexual underpinnings. While he played as a man possessed, he rolled his eyes toward the heavens, always wore a Hungarian sword at the piano, and kept two instruments on stage. If he broke one, he could leave it, like a spent lover, and move on to the next. Women fainted and men wept. He knew how to work a room, or rather, salon. He knew exactly what he was doing.

That covers the Sex and Music of the rock star image. As for the Drugs part of the formula, he was lifetime friends with Berlioz who indulged.

But the man was legitimately musically gifted. Liszt helped pave the way for 20th century music. He did not write symphonies in the Classical sense; he wrote symphonic poems, which were a programmatic cross between a Beethoven overture and a Berlioz symphony. His themes underwent TRANSFORMATIONS facilitated by his daring chromatic musical vocabulary. Technically, at the piano, he was a superior athlete, devising moves that baffle today's pianists. He gave the melody to the thumb, yet another innovation.

Chromaticism, using tones foreign to a given key, heightened the drama, increased the tension, and enabled a musical train of thought, free association, as had never been previously heard.

But if there is one word to be associated with Liszt it must be TRANSCRIPTION. Liszt is the acknowledged master of reworking non-piano compositions, such as a symphony, for the piano. He captured sounds exclusive to other instruments; brass, winds, strings, percussion. Nothing was lost in transcription. He unselfishly championed new music other than his own, bringing it to hundreds of Europeans who never would have heard it.

He made the piano a substitute orchestra.

Liszt was born in Hungary but felt a closer kinship to the French. His father – with that Leopold Mozart look in his eyes – dragged his 10-year old meal-ticket to Vienna where young Liszt studied with Czerny and, as legend has it, was kissed by Beethoven, who described him as a "Devil of a fellow – such a young rascal." A few rough years followed, but by the age of 16, young Liszt snapped out of it, returned to Paris with his mother, and became the new darling of the salons.

He became fascinated with a right-wing Catholic mystic named Abbé Lemennais from whom the composer/pianist got the concept of artist as priest. Religion aside (*WAY* aside), Liszt continued his sexcapades, having *ménages à trois* in snow-bound chateaux, and more famously, with a long-time amour named Marie, the Countess d'Agoult, who wrote literary works under the name of Daniel Stern.

Liszt and Marie had two daughters, Blandine and Cosima, the latter of whom ended up as the wife of Richard Wagner. Due to his continued philandering, Marie threw Liszt out, and he moved in with a Polish princess in Weimar. While there, Liszt put the city on the musical map, producing Wagner's operas, conducting the orchestra, and composing some of his most famous works. He ended up taking pseudo holy orders.

Working indefatigably, he was both festival director at Weimar and director of the New Hungarian Academy of Music in Budapest. He snuck one more affair into his busy schedule, which was starting to take its toll on his health. While on his way to see Wagner's *Tristan und Isolde* in Bayreuth, he caught a cold which turned into pneumonia and killed him a week later.

Greatest Hits:

> Symphonic:
> > *Les Préludes*
> > *Faust Symphony*
> > *Dante Symphony*
> > Two Piano Concertos

Piano Solos:
> Twenty *Hungarian Rhapsodies*
> Twelve *Transcendental Études*
> *Sonata* in B Minor

Johannes Brahms (1833-1897)

He was the last member of "The Three B's" of music: Bach, Beethoven, Brahms. He was so designated in his own lifetime. And he thought himself a man born too late.

He looked back to the Classical period by using its architectural forms, and reached back even farther by employing Baroque technical disciplines. Within this framework, Brahms injected the musically colorful scenery of German Romanticism.

Schumann loved him, calling him "the true Apostle."

Tchaikovsky called him a "scoundrel" and a "giftless bastard."

And so the battle lines were drawn.

Brahms was in direct opposition to the New German Romantic School of composition, championed by Liszt and Wagner – with whom things got rather nasty. They were the modernists of the Romantic era, and Brahms was the culminator of the great German Romantic tradition; picking up where Beethoven, Schubert, Schumann and even Bach, left off.

Today, we hear Brahms as infants; being lulled to sleep with a symphonic excerpt, affectionately called Brahms' "Lullaby." On television we see Roberta Flack as a child in Brooklyn, playing a Brahms *Intermezzo* on the piano for an AT & T ad. An orchestra's season would not be complete without one of his four symphonies programmed.

Born in Hamburg to a poor family, Brahms showed talent early on but initially studied law. He was offered a tour in America, but his piano teacher nixed the idea. Going to school and practicing, young Brahms made a meagre amount of money teaching piano. To supplement his income, he played in dance halls, taverns and restaurants in the seedy part of the city that catered to a huge navy base.

As a teenager he hooked up with a Hungarian violinist who loved Gypsy music – which was all the rage in Germany - and came into contact with a premier violinist who became Brahms' lifetime friend, Joseph Joachim. Brahms eventually met Liszt but found their views differed. He then went on to meet the Schumanns, who supported his music. Unfortunately, Robert Schumann had a nervous breakdown and attempted suicide, having to be put away for good. Over the years, Brahms became a good friend of Clara Schumann, but nothing ever came of it.

Shuttling between Hamburg and Detmold, Brahms composed – slowly. His works were well-received everywhere, except for Leipzig, the Liszt/Wagner stronghold. But Brahms got an appointment in Vienna, widened his circle of friends and composed his *German Requiem*. More and more popular compositions were making him and his publisher rich. He was well-liked, known to be thoughtful and generous, and loved food and wine. He received awards all over Europe.

In 1896 he was found to have hepatic cancer, but he chose to keep up his busy social calendar. A year later in April, he died.

Greatest Hits:

> Orchestral:
>> Four Symphonies
>> *Variations on a Theme by Haydn*
>> *Tragic Overture*
>> *Academic Festival Overture*
>> *Alto Rhapsody*
>
> Concertos:
>> *Violin concerto* in D
>> Two Piano Concertos
>
> Piano Music:
>> *Ballades*
>> *Intermezzi*
>> *Capriccios*

Rhapsodies
Variations and Fugue on a Theme
of Handel

Miscellaneous Chamber Music

Vocal Music:
German Requiem
Liebeslieder waltzes

Romantic Opera-tors

In the life-cycle of opera, the 19th century represents its prime. The majority of opera companies stock their repertory with the staples of the 1800's. While the genre had been around approximately two hundred years already, it was in the 19th century that it truly became music drama, with music reflecting the action and the emotions, and even representing characters and their entanglements.

And, in the true Romantic tradition, the composers led lives rivaled only by the plots of the operas they created.

ARTIST'S RENDERING OF INTERIOR OF
LA SCALA OPERA HOUSE

Virginia Bates

Gioacchino Rossini (1792-1868)

Ask a six-year old today who the Lone Ranger is and you will get a blank look.

But ask any Baby Boomer the same question and the driving rhythms of Rossini's *William Tell* overture will erupt from their lips as they bounce on horseback along with the masked, heroic cowboy, interjecting "Hi-ho Silver, and away!"

Chances are the six-year old will know excerpts from *The Barber of Seville*. Who can forget Bugs Bunny's interpretation of Figaro, the barber, as he shaves Elmer Fudd. During commercial breaks, the efficiency and speed of a cordless shaver is reflected in Figaro's frenzied phonetics of *Largo al factorum*.

These two operas represent the peak of Italian opera in the early 19th century; *William Tell* as grand opera, *Il barbiere di Siviglia* as *opera buffa* (comic opera). Rossini had revolutionized the genre in two ways: he filled out the orchestra, and he wrote out vocal embellishments for the singers which were previously left to chance.

Rossini, the man, remains somewhat of an enigma. He had success early on, being all the rage in Europe and especially Paris, all by the age of 37. He retired a rich man and devoted the rest of his life to food, wine, women and song. A youthful indiscretion left him with gonorrhea, which plagued him the rest of his life. Much decorated and greatly adored, Rossini nevertheless went into a severe depression. He never wrote another opera. His second wife helped him out of it, dragging him to Paris where they held famous Saturday *soirées*. He continued to compose little pieces. In 1858 his health deteriorated, and an operation revealed rectal cancer. He is buried in Santa Maria Novella in Florence.

Greatest Hits:

      Operas:

           William Tell

           *Il Barbiere di Siviglia (*The Barber of
               Seville*)*

La scala di seta (The Silken Ladder)

Tancredi

L'italiana in Algeri (The Italian Girl in
    Algiers)

Otello

La cenerentola (Cinderella)

La gazza ladra (The Thieving Magpie)

La donna del lago (The Lady of the Lake*)*

Richard Wagner (1813-1883)

When you think of *opera*, you think of a howling horned, braided blonde super-vixen, heaving her breast-plates and singing something that sounds like a foreign automobile import: "Toy-o-ta-ho!"

That is Wagner.

Vikings, vixens, legends and myths: 19th century audiences lapped it up; 20th century audiences lap it up, too. But in both centuries Wagner has inspired loathing as well as loving. In his own time, Wagner's intellectual nemesis was a critic named Eduard Hanslick. He also made enemies of Berlioz, Brahms, Schumann and Nietzsche, the last of whom called him "a disease" who "contaminates everything he touches." His followers, however, were and are fanatical about his operas. Wagner inspired extremes.

The crazy thing about Wagner is that he seriously studied musical composition after he decided to write operas – usually it is the other way around. He has been labeled "music-dramatist," not "composer." He was the first to write his own librettos, or stories. His greatest innovation was the *Leitmotiv*, a musical tag line. Each character, the relationships, a location, even a curse – all had recognizable jingles that Wagner brilliantly wove together into a tapestry of opera. Everything in the libretto had a musical parallel.

But what of this man, this genius who was so certain of his importance in human history that he began his autobiography as a youngster? Born in Leipzig, Wagner played the piano by ear and wrote essays and poems. He started writing plays but when he heard Weber's *Der Freischütz* and Beethoven's *Fidelio*, he realized music was the missing necessary element of his creativity. He found a teacher, and for the next several years bounced around trying to get his music performed and getting and losing conducting jobs. At one point he was thrown into debtors' prison. He married a leading lady but the union was a travesty.

Wagner's first significant opera was *Rienzi*, written when he was 29 years old. In 1843 the *Flying Dutchman* resulted from a stormy crossing to London from a Baltic port and is based on an old legend. *Tannhäuser* came two years later. By this time Wagner was becoming involved in German politics and religion. In 1847 he completed *Lohengrin*. In the next 25 years he mooched off friends and wrote three important works of prose, the most important of which was *Opera and Drama*. Meanwhile, back in Weimar, Liszt produced Wagner's operas, which were well-received.

The early 1850s saw the conception of the four-opera collection, *Der Ring des Nibelungen*. Twenty-six years and a couple of amours later, the great 90-leitmotiv tetralogy was produced in Bayreuth. In the interim, he completed *Tristan und Isolde*. He also hooked up with Cosima, the daughter of Liszt, and fathered a few offspring. In 1867, *Der Meistersinger* was finished. Thanks to the ardently admiring King Ludwig II, Wagner's dream – an enormous theater for opera and a Wagner festival which is still going strong and managed by family members – came true in Bayreuth. In 1880, Wagner finished his last opera, *Parsifal*. Most of his operas deal with the redemption of mortal passion through death.

His own death came in the form of a massive heart attack, and he drew his last breath in Cosima's arms.

Greatest Hits:

> *Overture to Rienzi*

> Operas:
>> *Der fliegende Holländer* (The Flying
>> Dutchman)

Tannhäuser

Lohengrin

Der Ring des Nibelungen

  which consists of:

  "Das Rheingold"

  "Die Walküre"

  "Siegfried"

  "Die Götterdammerung"

Tristan und Isolde

Die Meistersinger von Nürnberg

Parsifal

Giuseppe Verdi (1813-1901)

Verdi was the antithesis of Wagner.

He was a national hero; Wagner was banned from Germany.

He culminated the great Italian operatic tradition; Wagner reinvented German opera.

Verdi was a humanist; Wagner, a fantasist.

Verdi knew of Wagner; Wagner did not acknowledge Verdi's existence.

Verdi wrote melodies; Wagner engineered tag-lines.

Verdi used a slew of librettists; Wagner was his own.

The only thing they had in common was that they were born the same year, 1813.

Verdi wrote wonderful, singable melodies – an Italian phenomenon. They have been Madison Avenue favorites for years, authenticating any product trying to convey its Italianism such as pasta or pizza. In a non-ethnic usage, British Airways had a television ad in which an SST floats through space to the *"Va, pensiero"* chorus from *Nabucco*. It translates "Go, Thoughts".

And the sheer spectacle of Verdi can fill stadiums and coliseums around the world, as was proven in the late 1980's when *Aïda* toured with 35 live animals (elephants, camels, lions, tigers, leopards, horses, doves and a huge python), a cast of 1200, and enormous props recreating ancient Egypt. Switchboards in New York City were aglow when the 46-foot high Sphinx was sighted floating down the Hudson River toward the Statue of Liberty on a barge for delivery to the Meadowlands Sports Complex.

Spectacle aside, the most astonishing phenomenon about Verdi was that his operas gave hope and confidence to a broken and disparate Italy, so much in fact that it changed the course of history. What sort of a man could rally a country through an unlikely medium – opera?

Verdi grew up in a little village and took lessons from the local organist. By the age of 16 he was composing and conducting. Over the next several years he landed a conducting job, married and had two children who died with their mother following a few years later.

In 1842, at La Scala in Milan, Verdi's *Nabucco* triumphed. The Italians, plagued by the Austrians nipping at their provinces, rallied, identifying with the opera's political plot. And so, a national hero was born.

Verdi wrote twenty-six operas in all, most of which deal with humans in political situations, or humans in human situations. Who can forget the coughing courtesan, Violetta, as she hacks through *La Traviata*, the victim of tuberculosis who finds true love on her deathbed? Or, Verdi's clever observation of music in the workaday situation which he elevated, in the *"Anvil Chorus"* of *Il Trovatore*? At the age of seventy he wrote *Otello*, and at eighty, *Falstaff*.

In the late 1840s, Verdi found love again, with the soprano, Giuseppina Strepponi. They eventually married and adopted a little girl, calling her Maria. Verdi was mobbed and adored wherever he went. He relaxed on his farm, built a hospital, erected a home for aging musicians, and was appointed a senator in Rome. His wife died first, succumbing to pneumonia. Four years later in 1901, Verdi died of a stroke in Milan. A month later, the two bodies were moved to the musicians' rest home, with 100,000 fans lining the street. Toscanini led a chorus of 800 singing, *"Va, pensiero"*.

Greatest Hits:

Operas:
Aïda
Un Ballo in Maschera (A Masked Ball)
Don Carlos
Ernani
Falstaff
La Forza del Destino (The Force of
     Destiny)
Luisa Miller
Macbeth
Nabucco
Otello
Rigoletto
Simon Boccanegra
La Traviata (The Fallen Woman)
Il Trovatore (The Troubadour)

Vocal Music:
Requiem
Quattro pezzi sacri

Giacomo Puccini (1858-1924)

Gorgeous melody enjoying an unprecedented symbiosis with the score, prominent places on the rosters of every major opera house, audiences singing along, and yet...

"Too sappy," say some.

"All plot and no poetry," say others.

"Poor taste", "overt emotionalism", and "shabby little shocker" are some of the more colorful descriptions of Puccini's immensely popular operas.

Puccini's characters are real as are their situations. This treatment is called the "verist" school or *"verismo"*. This is a turnoff to cerebral traditionalists. But the audience can grasp the human condition, which accounts for Puccini's enormous popularity and staying power, in spite of what the critics may have said or do say.

Like Beethoven, Puccini straddles two eras, in this case it is the Romantic and the 20th century. Academics treat him primarily as a late Romantic composer – and the last in the great Italian opera tradition.

The fifth generation of musical Puccinis from Lucca, Italy, this composer got his big break in 1893, when his second work, *Manon Lescaut*, premiered in Turin. *La Bohème* came next in 1896, with a dazzling young conductor named Arturo Toscanini in the pit. *Tosca* sold out twenty houses in 1900 despite rumors of a bomb-threat the first night.

After obsessing about things Japanese (as was the fashion) for four years, *Madama Butterfly* debuted at La Scala. It was a disaster that needed re-writing and re-casting. Finally, it was a hit.

In 1906 Puccini and his wife crossed the Atlantic at the invitation of the Metropolitan Opera to see four of his most popular works performed there. His American sojourn gave him an idea for a new opera, which became *La Fanciulla del West*. It premiered at the Met in 1910, Toscanini conducted, Caruso sang, and there were fifty curtain calls.

Puccini suffered from throat cancer, and it finally killed him.

Greatest Hits:

Operas:
La Bohème (Bohemian Life)
Madama Butterfly
Tosca
Turandot
Manon Lescaut

La Fanciulla del West (The Girl of the
Golden West)
La Rondine (The Swallow)

One-act Operas:
Il Trittico (collection of three operas)
Gianni Schicchi
Suor Angelica (Sister Angelica)
Il Tabarro (The Cloak)

Virginia Bates

**ARTIST'S RENDERING OF EXTERIOR OF
OPERA HOUSE IN FRANKFURT, GERMANY**

The Late Heavies: Bruckner, Mahler and R. Strauss

Welcome to Late, Late Romantic Music. Sometimes it is so Late it is called Post-Romanticism. Bruckner, Mahler and Strauss are the Marathon Men of music composition. By the end of the 19th century, they and others were composing enormous pieces for the orchestra which tested the endurance of audiences, the conductor and the musicians themselves. These symphonic monsters were not simply the Classical embryo grown up; we are talking amoeba to T. Rex. But besides the obvious growth in size, the Marathon Men wrote pieces of greater complexity, expanded the musical language, demanded faster performing resources than ever before, and basically wreaked enough havoc to set the stage for the 20th Century.

It is all a matter of personal preference; either you love this music or you loathe it. It will smother you or elate you. For some, it is too much of a good thing; others cannot get enough. To survive a performance in the concert hall, one must be in top form: no liquids for at least two hours prior, a pasta meal beforehand (yes, even for breakfast), good working knowledge of isometric exercises, and today's and yesterday's New York Times crossword puzzles – with an erasable pen (no scratching pencils, please). Staying awake will be your greatest challenge. These pieces are L-O-N-G.

When a major symphony orchestra is in the throes of Mahler, however, it can be the thrill of a lifetime.

You must judge for yourself.

Anton Bruckner (1824-1896)

He has been called "the most noble figure of the 19th century" and "a half-wit."

His symphonies begin out of thin air with raindrops of sound, and work themselves into full-blown musical typhoons. And they are permeated by his religious spirit. Their design has been called cathedral-like in proportion – having the sound of a huge pipe organ.

Poor Bruckner. In Vienna, where he eventually ended up as a professor of harmony, organ and counterpoint, he made a huge political error: he worshipped Wagner. Brahms, a passionate anti-Wagnerian, labeled Bruckner's orchestral works, "symphonic boa-constrictors".

He did gain notoriety and respect for his virtuosity at the organ and his stunning talent in composition, particularly counterpoint, which is a discipline of composition, literally, "note against note". He won over the emperor of his native Austria, being named to the Order of Franz Joseph. When his health began to deteriorate in the 1890s, the emperor provided a gatekeeper's lodge for him. He made numerous proposals, but died a virgin.

His music was so innovative, that he has been pegged as a Post-Romantic composer.

Greatest Hits:

Symphonies:

Bruckner wrote nine symphonies: the most popular are the 4th, 7th, 8th and 9th

Religious music:

Mass in C Major

Requiem

Te Deum

Cantata:

Helgoland

Gustav Mahler (1860-1911)

Only now, more than eighty years after his death, is the public getting fanatical about Mahler.

Mahler is now selling out concerts.

Mahler conducted by Leonard Bernstein and captured on compact disc is now a coveted possession.

And yes, even now, Mahler's music is moving out of the graveyard shift on Classical radio, and into prime time.

Like scotch, Mahler is an acquired taste; intolerable at first, and later, an indulgence.

On paper, the Austrian's compositional output looks anemic; nine full symphonies and an incomplete tenth, and some song cycles. But set the timer and your hair will start to go grey before the last note is sounded. Considering he composed only during the summers between conducting commitments, his achievement borders on the superhuman.

But once again we have the case of the "Misunderstood Composer". An abrasive personality, intolerance for lack of talent and an obsession with perfection kept him bouncing from one conducting post to another – including the Metropolitan Opera and New York Philharmonic Society. Whenever his compositions were performed with him or someone else on the podium, the critics pulverized him – in some cases simply because he was born Jewish. Fortunately, there was no question the man was a virtuoso conductor, so he always had a place to go.

Until later in his life, he usually went alone. True love eluded him as did favorable press. The 42-year old Mahler was finally smitten by a 23-year old beauty named Alma, who could stand up to his antics. They went to the altar expecting their first child in 1902. Things turned sour after the death of one of their two children from scarlet fever. Alma needed to recover at a rest home, her husband went off conducting, and she met Walter Gropius, the famous architect whom she later married in 1915. Before that happened, however, she had affairs and another marriage. A discriminating woman, she only slept with geniuses. For a while she and Mahler were in therapy with Sigmund Freud.

As far as pegging Mahler in a music-history context, most experts agree he reached a turning point in his *Fifth Symphony* in which he waved good-bye to the 19th Century once and for all. In the tradition of Beethoven, Mahler incorporated voices into his Second, Third, Fourth and Eighth symphonies. The *Eighth Symphony* is also known as the "Symphony of a Thousand" because it calls for eight soloists, a double chorus, boys' choir, organ and a gigantic orchestra. Another large-scale work is *Das Lied von der Erde*. It is a song cycle for two soloists and a large orchestra based on a Chinese text translated into German. This exemplifies his being known as the "song symphonist".

Mahler is considered to be the last of the great German symphonists, in a tradition generated by Haydn and Mozart, and furthered by Beethoven, Schubert, Schumann, Brahms and Bruckner.

Mahler said: "To write a symphony for me is to construct a world." Whether a world of Nature, a world of the spiritual or a world resigned to death, his symphonies are intensely expressive and subjective – and programmatic.

Mahler died at midnight on May 18, 1911 at the age of 50 from strep and progressive heart failure. He was said to have muttered "Mozart" as the thunder crashed outside.

Greatest Hits:

> Nine Symphonies
> Song Cycles:
>> *Das Lied von der Erde* (Song of the Earth)
>> *Lieder eines fahrenden Gesellen* (Songs of
>>> the Wayfarer)
>> *Kindertotenlieder* (Children's Death
>> Songs)
>> *Das Knaben Wunderhorn* (The Youth's
>> Magic Horn)

Richard Strauss (1864-1949)

"I employ cacophony to outrage people," Strauss once said.

Outrage, he did.

The composer, Cesar Cui, commented in 1904, "His absurd cacophony will not be music even in the 30th century."

Claude Debussy, the French Impressionist composer, said of *Till Eulenspiegel*, " This piece might be called 'An hour of original music in a lunatic asylum.' "

And the great German composer, Paul Hindemith, said of one of Strauss' symphonies in 1917, "Better to hang oneself than ever to write music like that."

German-born, he is unrelated to the waltzing Strausses of Vienna.

Richard Strauss was catapulted into present-day fame when the film, *2001: A Space Odyssey*, hit the theaters in 1968. The haunting imagery of the astronaut drifting in space with Strauss' heroic and explosive excerpt from his symphonic poem, *Thus Spake Zarathustra*, has come to signify the inherent drama of outer space itself. In a subsequent television ad, the astronaut has been replaced by a high-tech electric toothbrush.

Strauss has become known for his symphonic poems and several highly-successful operas. In his early years as a composer near the end of the 19th century, Strauss was profoundly affected upon hearing the music of Wagner and Liszt. Trademarks of his extremist style include churning horns, brass fanfares, loud soaring strings, and big-time gloom.

After some decades of writing symphonic poems, Strauss turned to opera, and in 1905 hit home runs with *Salome* and *Elektra*. In 1911 came his most popular opera, *Der Rosenkavalier* . He had a twenty-year working relationship with the librettist, Hugo von Hofmannsthal.

In Strauss' later years he was both admired and snubbed because of his egomania and the materialism and eroticism in his operas. He passed away in Munich and his wife followed him eight months later.

Greatest Hits:

> *Symphonic Poems:*
> > *Death and Transfiguration*
> > *Thus Spake Zarathustra*
> > *Till Eulenspiegel's Merry Pranks*
> > *Don Juan*
>
> *Operas:*
> > *Arabella*
> > *Ariadne auf Naxos*
> > *Capriccio*
> > *Elektra*
> > *Salome*
> > *Die Frau ohne Schatten*
> > *Der Rosenkavalier* (The Knight of the Rose)
>
> Two Horn Concertos
>
> *Metamorphosen for Strings*

Neo, Geo, and Where Do We Go From Here?

(Transition between centuries)

As you can imagine, in one hundred years' time there are certainly more composers to talk about than those already highlighted in this chapter. Toward the end of the 19th century, composers were going off in different directions, creatively. Some infused their national traits into their music, others went for more universal appeal. Some stuck to traditional formats, others ignored them. Things were going to extremes; in length, in subject matter, in harmony.

And it drives music historians crazy trying to neatly pigeon-hole these highly individual composers. It is a transitional time, to say the least.

For the sake of simplicity, the following composers have been organized by country – whether they subscribed to Nationalism in their music or Universalism or eroticism for that matter!

CZECH REPUBLIC

Antonín Dvořák (1841-1904)

Wrote nine symphonies, the most popular being the *Ninth* or *New World Symphony* and which referred to the composer's first trip to the United States. It was premiered by the New York Philharmonic in 1893. Also frequently programmed is a terrific *Concerto for Cello*. His style is middle of the road Romantic, with influences from polka rhythms, Czech folk music and dances. His work is sometimes labeled "Brahmsian".

ENGLAND

Sir Edward Elgar (1857-1934)

What graduate has not processed to the solemn, academic orchestral march from Elgar's *Pomp and Circumstance*? Not since Purcell (remember him from the Baroque period?), has England produced so thoroughly a British composer. Elgar's *Enigma Variations* are especially clever, with all kinds of literary allusions.

FRANCE

As in the past, France was a fertile country for music.

Camille Saint-Saëns (1835-1921)

He poked fun at the sappy Romantic compositions, preferring French restraint and dignity. His *Piano Concerto No.4* is a repertoire staple. Wanting to be taken seriously, he did not allow the colorful and witty *Carnival of the Animals* to be performed or published in his lifetime. The first performance was given two months after his death. Ironically, it is his most celebrated piece!

Leo Delibes (1836-1891)

Starting out as a church organist, he found the stage and made a name for himself composing operas and ballets. *Coppelia* is at the core of every ballet-lover's heart. After Tchaikovsky heard a performance of *Coppelia*, he despondently wrote to a friend that he felt ashamed of his own ballets, so beautiful was Delibes' music. His opera, *Lakme*, considered to be his masterpiece, has been frequently tapped by ad-types for numerous campaigns ranging from airlines to perfume, usually excerpting the beautifully haunting *"Bell Song"*.

Georges Bizet (1838-1875)

He started off with a bang as a 10-year old musical *wunderkind*, and nearly ended with a whimper. Most of his compositions from adulthood were not well-received in his lifetime. But the brilliant opera comique, *Carmen,* was enjoying its thirty-first performance the night Bizet died – a very good run indeed. With its passion, drama, and seductive Mediterranean lustiness, *Carmen* remains one of the most popular operas ever written.

Gabriel Fauré (1845-1924)

As a pupil of Saint-Saëns, he is best known for his pieces written on an intimate scale: chamber works, songs and piano works. He really cannot be pegged as a Romantic composer. Wagner-loathers gravitate to Fauré. His musical vocabulary was influenced by his in-depth study of Gregorian chant accompaniment, with the modality finding its way into his melodies. (See page 143 for more on this century-straddler.)

NORWAY

Edvard Grieg (1843-1907)

His *Peer Gynt Suite* No. 1 remains ever popular, with its *"In the Hall of the Mountain King"* and *"Anitra's Dance"* being the most often-heard excerpts. His *Piano Concerto* is an important concert standard. Influenced by Norwegian folksongs and dances, Grieg's style is a blending of these rhythms and modalities giving his music lyrical, atmospheric and impressionistic qualities. His life inspired a 1945 Broadway musical called *Song of Norway.*

RUSSIA

Another hot-bed of creativity!

Modest Mussorgsky (1839-1881)

Russian accents and folksongs get lots of references in his vivid and colorful works. *A Night on Bald Mountain* is a swirling wonder, and *Pictures at an Exhibition,* a piano piece, creeps into modern pop music now and then, particularly as orchestrated by Ravel. The four-act music drama, *Boris Godunov,* gained popularity (like *A Night on Bald Mountain*) after Rimsky-Korsakov revised it. His output uneven and frequently incomplete, Mussorgsky suffered from alcoholism which killed him.

Peter Ilyich Tchaikovsky (1840-1893)

All over the United States on or around Independence Day, orchestras traditionally play Tchaikovsky's *1812 Overture.* With its church bells, cannon shots and familiar themes, it is as stirring for Americans as it is for Russians; the work having been written to commemorate the latters' defeat of Napoleon's armies that year. The composer did not care for this piece very much. *The Nutcracker* ballet, another perennial favorite, is so mainstream as to be ubiquitous at Christmas time. It represents, however, the first time a *celesta* (a keyboard instrument that plays bell sounds) is included in an orchestral score (think Sugar Plum Fairy). His other greatest hits include: the opera, *Eugene Onegin*; the ballet, *Swan Lake;* the Third, Fifth and Sixth symphonies; *Second Piano Concerto* and the *Violin Concerto.* And what toddler cannot sing along with Disney's enchanting animated classic of 1959 *Sleeping Beauty* which is soundtracked by the Russian master's ballet of the same name.

Nikolai Rimsky-Korsakov (1844-1908)

Fantasy, bright musical coloration and orientalism characterize this composer's music. . Listen to the glittering symphonic suite, *Scheherazade*. He wrote the book on orchestration and was the teacher of Igor Stravinsky.

**THE MUSIC WORLD OF
EUROPE IN 1856**

Photodisc

Slingspiel*

Does it seem as though when Romantic composers were not composing, they were hurling insults at one another? See if you can match the composer to the insulting quote.

The barbs are remarkably interchangeable, so do not get discouraged.

1. Berlioz	a. "Old Borax"
	James Huneker
2. Brahms	b. "Giftless bastard"
	Tchaikovsky
3. Bruckner	c. "A monster"
	Debussy
4. Chopin	d. "An inspired charlatan"
	Hermann Levi
5. Dvořák	e. "A tragic case"
	Nadia Boulanger
6. Elgar	f. "Astounding lack of talent"
	Tchaikovsky
7. Liszt	g. "One of the Seven Humbugs of Christendom"
	Shaw
8. Sibelius	h. "A morbidly sentimental flea"
	J.W. Davison
9. Strauss	i. "That old poisoner"
	Debussy
10. Tchaikovsky	j. "Music that stinks to the ear"
	Eduard Hanslick
11. Wagner	k. "A half-wit"
	Hans von Bülow

* *NOTE*: "Slingspiel" is a take on *singspiel*, a type of 18th century German opera with a lot of dialogue.

Slingspiel Answers

Answers: 1.c., 2.b., 3.k., 4.h., 5.a., 6.g., 7. d., 8.e., 9.f., 10.j., 11.i.

Test Your R. Q.

(Romantic Quotient)

Decide whether a statement is true or false:

1. *Bagatelle* is a pocketbook boutique on Madison Avenue.
2. *Capriccio* is the newest java concoction, originating in truck-stops in the Pacific Northwest.
3. *Idée fixe* is a tasting menu at a set price in a three star restaurant.
4. *Lied* is the past tense of lie, as in fib.
5. *Leitmotiv* refers to the cause of petty crime; as opposed to *heavymotiv*.
6. *Les Troyens* is an opera about practitioners of safe sex.
7. *Rubato* is a fast massage. It can also be the masseur's name.
8. *Nabucco* is an oriental cookie company.
9. A KLM pilot is the subject of Wagner's opera, *The Flying Dutchman*.
10. A *cadenza* is a coveted piece of office furniture.

Test Your R.Q. Answers

(Answers to True / False statements)

You have probably deduced that all the statements are *false*. Here are the words defined.

1. *Bagatelle* – a short little piece, usually for piano.
2. *Capriccio* – a whimsical, free-form instrumental piece.
3. *Idée fixe* – literally "fixed idea"; the buzzword for Berlioz' recurring theme.
4. *Lied* – literally "song", in this case, referring to art-song.
5. *Leitmotiv* – in Wagner's operas, a musical tag-line.
6. *Les Troyens* – an opera by Berlioz.
7. *Rubato* – literally "robbed". The melody slows down for dramatic effect, then accelerates, thus *robbing* the notes of their full time values. Mostly associated with Chopin.
8. *Nabucco* – an opera by Verdi.
9. *Flying Dutchman* – an opera by Wagner.
10. *Cadenza* – a fancy, elaborate passage usually played at the end of the first and/or third movement of concertos, which features a solo instrument. Cadenza-like passages are integrated into some other compositions for a quick burst of virtuosic playing - just to keep the audience awake.

Movement 6

The 20th Century: Anything Goes!

"Nowadays, HARMONY comes almost as a shock."

Kathleen Raine

"Modern music is as dangerous as cocaine."

Pietro Mascagni

Movement 6

The 20th Century - Anything Goes!

If you have ever wondered what that intermittent rumbling was on weekends, it is the stampeding herds of frightened concert-goers escaping an aural confrontation with 20th Century music. Despite the fact that music directors have no choice but to cleverly slip 20th Century compositions into the program between crowd-pleasing classics, audiences still find creative ways to exit the concert hall in droves to avoid being subjected to a piece written after December 31, 1899.

And in some instances, their flight is justified. A quick cappuccino would taste better than the occasional bitter pill on the program. During most concerts, however, audience members – many of them quite seasoned – are missing out on a future classic because of a simple fear of the unknown or a case of closed-mindedness.

It is all a matter of getting used to, acquainting the ear to the new musical language, sound and ideas. Music that was scandalous in the century's infancy, is now mainstream. Case in point: The debut of Igor Stravinsky's *Rite of Spring* in Paris, in 1913, caused a riot because of its so-called "barbaric" rhythms and innovative use of tonality. It hit a powerful nerve in the collective psyche of the audience and stirred the emotions. Even today, it still quickens the pulse and can make you a bit dizzy – like a strong cup of coffee – but will not cause a heart attack, just a pleasant buzz.

Music of this century can be fascinating, amusing, and absurd. Why, even a tin-eared number-cruncher can get a lot out of some pieces because his visceral reactions will correspond to numerical progressions or statistical maneuverings. For example, he will experience the Fibonacci series* at work in Ernst Krenek's *Fibonacci-Mobile* premiered in 1965.

John Cage taught us to consider the sonic inversion of music – *silence*. Instead of the musical photograph, he shows us the negative. But that emerges into a new picture; silence is full of sound! In his 1954 piece entitled *4' 33"*, a pianist sits at the piano for the duration – and does not play a single note. The audience thus considers the non-piano sounds in the venue, even their own breathing or rumbling stomachs.

George Crumb integrated new sources of sounds such as toy pianos and Tibetan prayer stones into his 1970 composition called *Ancient Voices of Children.* He altered the characters of traditional orchestral instruments by placing paper between harp strings or bending the pitch of a piano string with a chisel, for example.

Think of the new instruments at our disposal (yes, even the Dispose-All itself can play); computer-generated sounds, electronics of all kinds – any noisemaker can participate. Composers have integrated tapes, radios and computers into their pieces. Old instruments are given new treatment. Sounds can be synthesized, amplified, pre-recorded, mutated (mutilated) and oscillated.

Ironically, many New Music phobics have had experiences with some of these compositions – and do not even know it.

Grammy Award-winning pop artist, Sting, integrates a 1930s theme by Sergei Prokofiev in a song called *"Russians"*.

The movie, *Platoon,* has evocative music by Samuel Barber: his 1938 *Adagio for Strings.*

* *NOTE:* Fibonacci Series: Each number is the sum of its two antecedents, i.e. 1, 2, 3, 5, 8, 13, 21...

An innovative TV commercial for a new Oldsmobile is backed by an excerpt from Aaron Copland's 1944 ballet, *Appalachian Spring.*

For you aging hippies, Emerson, Lake & Palmer had a field day with Prokofiev's 1937 *Lieutenant Kije* suite.

United Airlines returns a businesswoman/mother home in time to tuck her daughter into bed to the strains of Gershwin's *Rhapsody in Blue* of 1924.

The action in the steamy movie *Dreamlover* (1994) is reinforced by the libidinous rhythms of Stravinsky's *Rite of Spring,* (1913).

Those are just a few mainstream examples.

To our Western-oriented (as opposed to Eastern) ears, the Classical triumvirate of Haydn, Mozart and Beethoven will always feel like the Home Base of Serious Music. Everything else was either going toward them or is moving away from them. But here is an interesting notion to ponder:

Many so-called "new" ideas have been drawn from or inspired by music from other cultures, such as the ragas of India or the five-note scales (*slendro*) of the Javanese. Ritual music of the natives of Micronesia sounds downright cutting-edge. These ethnomusics with their unique structures have been around for centuries – perhaps millennia. Yet they are alien to most of us. Conversely, our ditty, *"Mary Had a Little Lamb",* could sound like fingernails scratching a blackboard to a culture inhabiting an obscure peninsula of Siberia, or to the Maori of New Zealand.

As our global village grows more interactive, so will the traditional folk music of its cultures. American popular music already reflects its cultural melting pot; Latin, *reggae*, and ragas of India have found their way into the Top 40. Composers have always turned to their own cultures for inspiration. In the 20th Century and beyond, composers of "serious" music have and will continue to integrate these unique voices into their pieces. Perhaps what will emerge will be GLOBAL MUSIC or a global style: a step beyond international styles of the past (which really encompassed only a few countries in Europe).

This implies a blending of many styles and cultural idioms done by Cuisinart as opposed to a wooden spoon.

At the other end of the spectrum is ABSOLUTE MUSIC, music for its own sake. Composers have been tinkering with different systems of organization and shattering traditional harmony such as that found in Haydn, Mozart and Beethoven. Earlier in the 20th Century, Arnold Schoenberg developed Twelve-Tone music, with its own set of rules, and in which each tone received equal weight and importance. In the twilight of the century, Pulitzer Prize winner, George Perle, (b.1915) is developing *chromatic tonality*: a system using all twelve available notes in the chromatic scale (black and white keys on a piano, for example) but with a hierarchy similar to that of traditional "keys" and their seven-note scales.

What does 20th Century music sound like? It runs the gamut from lush and lyrical to stark and ugly. It is about possibilities. It mirrors the fast-forward pace of the century. It reflects politics and technology: the atomic age, the nuclear age and the cyber-age. It protests against all those things and celebrates them. It is not one thing, one aesthetic.

People have never been so afraid of their own music.

But like landing in a foreign country where initially the language is at odds with one's own, slowly the ear becomes acclimated, recognizing recurring rhythms, patterns and nuances, until it is no longer strange and unpleasant. Ironically, eventually one welcomes the exoticism, and even seeks it out.

Schoenberg's disciple, Anton Webern, who died in 1945 in Austria when mistakenly shot by a jittery 19-year old American military policeman when Webern lit a match during a blackout, once said of his own compositional output: "In fifty years one will find it obvious, children will understand it and sing it."

It just takes getting used to, and having an open mind. Why, the emperor of Austria once criticized Mozart for using "too many notes".

On Clapping for the Contemporary

The same rules apply in the concert venue for 20th Century music performances. Like their ancestors, a great number of these pieces are divided into movements and, therefore,

NO CLAPPING IS DONE BETWEEN THEM!

However, since rules are made to be broken – and nearly every rule lies maimed in the 20th Century – do pay close attention to how a piece is introduced or what is written about it in the program. Sometimes it is difficult to tell when a 20th Century piece is actually over; the familiar signals are not always there. Wait until the conductor turns completely around to face the audience, or for the performers to stand up and/or line up for a bow.

Who knows... the composer may WANT you to clap at odd times, thereby making you a performer and enriching your experience as audience!

A Century of -ISTs and Their -ISMs
or

What will the music history experts say about the 20th Century the farther they get away from it? Say, in 2025? Will it remain a hundred-year entity or be divided? Who will they highlight, who will they condemn? Who will emerge from the shadows, who will fade into obscurity? How will they be classified, pigeon-holed or nicknamed? What will music be like in 2025?

These are the composers to start with:

Igor Stravinsky (1882-1971)

The Titan of the Twentieth. Russian-American. Epitome of the century. Reinvented himself more often than Madonna. Great listening.

Claude Debussy (1862-1918)

The French Impressionist. His *Cathédrale Engloutie* actually sounds like a submerged cathedral. Century straddler.

John Cage (1912-1992)

Still the most outrageous, imaginative American composer. Roll the dice, compose a piece.

Aaron Copland (1900-1990)

Archetypal American. His music is the Grand Canyon and the Shakers, and even pushes beef and Oldsmobiles on TV.

Arnold Schoenberg (1874-1951)

Singularly responsible for obliterating traditional harmony once and for all, in 1910. Austrian-American. Fathered Serialism in the 1920's.

Charles Ives (1874-1954)

The New England Transcendentalist, the true anti-European. And a good businessman.

128

Philip Glass (1937-)

The American Minimalist. Calculated repetition. And quite successful at that. Has crossed over into mainstream acceptance, particularly with opera..opera..opera..opera.. opera.

These are the Founding Fathers of 20th Century Music. They are the serialists, expressionists, minimalists, transcendentalists, neo-classicists, anti-rationalists: practitioners of highly individualized interpretations of music composition. Some crossed into new areas. Like Picasso with his creative periods, a number of composers rejected and explored, threw out and innovated. Many carry more than one label. From them have grown numerous branches of composition, more schools than what fish travel around in, more branches than Citibank, more cross-overs than the National Hockey League.

It is a love-hate relationship with audiences and 20th Century music. New compositions enjoyed a surge in popularity for a while – being indiscriminately performed and programmed. The fact of the matter is that people realized, while brilliant on paper (or on the computer), it did not translate aurally very well. In fact, subway brakes would be more welcomed compared to some of the modern stuff. A free concert was one thing but to actually lay out hard-earned cash to be subjected to some of the truly mediocre stuff was intolerable. During his tenure as musical director of the New York Philharmonic, Pierre Boulez, trying to bring his subscribers into the 20th Century, instead succeeded in driving many away. So in the waning days of the 20th Century, concert programmers and ticket-buyers alike have become informed and careful about what to sell and what to buy; to sift out the good new music from the not-so-good. And try to second-guess each other.

But new music needs a forum. It appears to be gaining momentum again, due in part – ironically – to Mr. Boulez' doings in Paris – which have been well-received internationally – and probably the restlessness of audiences needing their aural intellects stimulated. New music concerts designated as such are growing in popularity. There are groups which specialize in the performance of 20th Century music only – and are gaining a loyal following.

There really is no tidy labelling of 20th Century music in a way that gives a clue to what the music is collectively about. The 19th Century is Romantic. The 18th Century is Classical. The 17th is Baroque. The 15th and 16th Centuries are the Renaissance. Only the Medieval period falls back on its historical designation. This parallel is a bit disturbing. Do we find ourselves in yet another Dark Ages? An era of creative turmoil or worse, floundering? If so, and if history is in fact repeating itself, take heart: we have Renaissance II, The Sequel, to look forward to.

What signposts do we look for in this span of one hundred years to understand the creative significance (or ridiculousness) of what has been and is being written?

Simply put, it is a century of -ISMs:

An -ISM is a theory or system, in this case, applied to musical composition. And the list below represents such legitimate systems, principles and schools of the 20th Century in music. Some are more catch-all than others. But an -ISM serves the purpose of description. Conveniently, if the -ISM does not exist, make up a new one. After all, it is the 20th Century we are talking about. And in the words of that great Yale tunesmith of the1930s, Cole Porter, "Anything Goes!"

Here are the most prominent of the -ISMs:

Serial-ISM

Atonal-ISM

Minimal-ISM

Impression-ISM

Expression-ISM

Neo-classic-ISM

Avant-garde-ISM

Anti-rational-ISM

Neo-Romantic-ISM

Transcendental-ISM.

The -ISM Makers or Who's Got -ISM?

Within each -ISM, the most important composers will be mentioned. Some fit into more than one as they experimented with different types of compositional approaches.

Understandably, composers do not like to be labeled (particularly when they are alive). Gian Carlo Menotti, when told that Donald Jay Grout designated him as a "born theatre composer of the order of Puccini and the verismo school," in his lengthy but diminutively-named textbook, *A Short History of Opera*, responded by autographing the inside cover as follows: "A stupid book - as far as I am concerned!"

SERIALISM

Arnold Schoenberg was its creator in 1923, with Alban Berg (1885-1935) and Anton Webern (1883-1945) his students and eventual masters in their own right. These three Austrian-born composers have been designated the Second Viennese School. The system is based on an arrangement or series of twelve tones (all the black and white keys without duplication of notes) which serve as the theme of a composition. All the twelve pitches have to appear in a specified order before the "row" of twelve notes can be repeated. Schoenberg's *Piano Pieces,* Op. 23 was the breakthrough composition.

Berg's vocabulary was more emotional than that of his teacher and integrated aspects of 17th, 18th and 19th century music. His *Violin Concerto* (1937) contains a direct quote of a hymn melody used by J. S. Bach in his *Cantata* No. 60 – as part of the twelve-tone "theme".

Webern expanded the twelve-tone system to include rhythm, dynamics and tone colors. Yet, his music is characterized by Classical sensibilities: brevity, clarity and delicacy. His 1924 *Drei Geistliche Volkslieder* (Three Spiritual Folksongs) is such an example.

Later in the century, the Frenchman, Pierre Boulez (b. 1925), and the German composer, Karlheinz Stockhausen (b. 1928), proved to be the ultra-serialists – musical control freaks if you will – imposing strict order on absolutely everything in the composition, even aspects such as density and difficulty. Boulez, who had been conductor of the New York Philharmonic and the Cleveland Orchestra, used electronic instruments to perform his serial compositions. Boulez is still going strong in Paris leading the avant-garde music scene there and taking it on the road as well. Stockhausen, who used tapes and electronics, has pushed serialism – which included directions to performers(!) – so far that it has become something else, something new, something not neatly labeled...yet.

Other total serializers or post-serializers include Milton Babbitt (b. 1916) with his *Concerti for Violin, Small Orchestra, and Synthesized Tape* (1976), Elliott Carter (b. 1908) who expanded the twelve-tone concept and developed "metric modulation" in *Double Concerto* (1951) and the Italian composer, Luigi Dallapiccola (1904-1975), who sent a message of liberty in his *Songs of Prison* (1941).

Even the mighty Stravinsky dabbled in serialism after 1948: *Threni* (1958), *Movements for Piano and Orchestra* (1959) and *Requiem Canticles* (1966).

Greatest Hits of the Serialists:

Arnold Schoenberg:
Verklärte Nacht (Transfigured Night),
Op. 4
Five Orchestra Pieces, Op. 16
Variations for Orchestra, Op. 31
A Survivor From Warsaw, Op. 4

Note: Only pieces marked Opus 23 and later are composed in the serial method.

Alban Berg:
Lyric Suite
Violin Concerto
Lulu
Wozzeck

Anton Webern:
Five Pieces for Orchestra, Op. 10

Symphony, Op. 21
Pierre Boulez:
Le Marteau sans Maître
(not ultra-rational)

Karlheinz Stockhausen:
Moment (1958)

ATONALISM

This is a catch-all term also known as atonality, that can be interpreted in a wide range, from a little bit of messing around with traditional tonality to its total obliteration. It seems to have begun with the late works of Sir Edward Elgar, Richard Strauss and Jean Sibelius at the turn of the 20th Century and was established once and for all by Schoenberg and his students' and followers' pre-serial works. Just about everything in the 20th Century that is not serial music but is clearly toying with *traditional tonality* can be labeled ATONAL.

MINIMALISM

Philip Glass is the most famous and mainstream of its practitioners. With its roots in the trance-inspiring music of Africa, Bali and India, minimalism is characterized by seemingly unending repetition in a relentless beat, with subtle changes over a prolonged period of time. La Monte Young, Terry Riley (not the basketball coach) and Steve Reich also composed in this style which caught the public's attention in the 1970s with Mr. Glass' opera, *Einstein on the Beach*.

Greatest Hits:

Einstein on the Beach (1976)
Satyagraha (1980)
Akhnaten (1984)

IMPRESSIONISM

The Frenchman, Claude Debussy, was the chief propo-
nent of this style, which like the blurred lines of his compatriot
artists in the late 1800s, blurred the music through the use of
chromaticism, modality and lush harmonies to suggest a mood.
The first to exploit the exotic sounding whole-tone scale, he
helped pave the way for the 20th Century. Heavy Pedal!

Greatest Hits:

> *Prelude to the Afternoon of a Faun*
> (1892-94)

Opera:

> *Pelléas et Mélisande* (1902)

Nocturnes (1897-99)

La mer (1903-5)

Images pour orchestre (1905-12)

Ballet:

> *Jeux* (1912-13)

Piano solo music:

> *Voiles*
>
> *La Cathédrale engloutie*

Also landing in this category are the French composers
Maurice Ravel and Erik Satie, although they had evolved their
own styles. Ravel, who had many works of note, is best known
for his 1928 tour de force, *Bolero*. His style is rooted in Classicism's structures and steady rhythms but is bathed in Impres-
sionism. He was a master colorist, using the orchestra as an
entirely new palette. Others of his hits include: *Rapsodie
espagnole*, (1907-8), *Daphnis et Chloé* (1909-12), *Le tombeau de
Couperin* (1917), *La valse* (1919-20), *Piano Concerto* in D major
for left hand (1929-30), *Concerto for Piano and Orchestra* in G
major (1929-31).

Erik Satie has been called an anti-impressionist, but
the orchestration of his 1888 *Gymnopédies* by his friend,
Claude Debussy, earned the piece a following. Unsentimental
and working irony and dry wit into his music, Satie earned

fame for his outrageous titles, *Dried Embryos* or *Three Pieces in the Shape of a Pear*. He rejected Baroque, Classical and Romantic norms by using a modal vocabulary, quoting cafe music, and underpinning it all with obsessive rhythms. The ballet, *Parade,* (1917) is one of his most famous large-scale works and incorporates mechanical devices such as a siren.

EXPRESSIONISM

Expressionism refers to what man was feeling inside. As it relates to the 20th Century, it means isolation, helplessness, tension, anxiety, fear and rebellion against the established. Béla Bartók and Paul Hindemith are considered to be outstanding expressionists. Arnold Schoenberg and Alban Berg (remember them from Serialism?) were also proponents. The effect was achieved through use of ATONALITY; not harmonious but terribly dissonant, fragmented, rhythmically uneven. Very effective when done right as in Schoenberg's: *Erwartung, Die glückliche Hand* and *Pierrot Lunaire*. Of his pupil, Alban Berg, the best are: *Lyric Suite*, and the operas, *Wozzeck* and *Lulu*, in the 1920s and 1930s.

NEO-CLASSICISM

This is another one of those big catch-all-ISMs. It refers to a style used by 20th Century composers who brought back Classical forms and symmetry and the classical treatment of themes, among other aspects. Within the classical forms, however, the musical vocabulary can range from tonal to not so tonal. Falling into this category are: the Swiss composer, Arthur Honegger (1892-1955), and the Frenchmen, Darius Milhaud (1892-1974), Francis Poulenc (1899-1963) and Olivier Messiaen (1908-1992). Messiaen's *Quartet for the End of Time* received its first performance in 1941 while the composer was in a prison camp.

Also in this category: Paul Hindemith (1895-1963), the German-American who left his country in 1940 because Hitler's government did not care for his early atonal works. Later, he wrote in a more tonal language based on the manipulation of tension and relaxation.

Greatest Hits:

> *Mathis der Maler* (1938)
> *Das Marienleben* (1923)
> *Variations on a Theme of Carl Maria von*
> *Weber*

Opera:

> *Cardillac* (1926)

The Russian, Sergei Prokofiev (1891-1953), an *enfant terrible* was all over the board stylistically, but remains primarily a neo-Classicist. His music's characteristics are: percussive, aggressive, dynamic, mechanistic. His *Peter and the Wolf* (1934), written in two weeks for children, is a symphonic fairy tale which also instructs about the orchestra. In the *Classical Symphony* (1918) he wrote in a modern language but used a traditional format. *Lieutenant Kijé* is a symphonic suite from a Russian film score, first performed in Paris in 1937 with Prokofiev leading the orchestra. The score was recycled in 1959 for the movie, *The Horse's Mouth.* His 1921 opera, *The Love for Three Oranges,* and *Symphony* No. 5 (1945) and *Symphony* No. 7 (1952) are among his most popular works as well.

Prokofiev's compatriot, Dmitri Shostakovich (1906-1975), was also under the Communist gun creatively. As long as he wrote in a traditional style, he was a celebrated composer. However, when he became more adventurous, his works were censored and labeled bourgeois and decadent. His string quartets are particularly extraordinary.

But, it is Igor Stravinsky – the most important, influential composer of the century – with whom the term, Neo-Classicism is identified; that is, for his works AFTER 1923. This Russian-American dabbled in colorful Russian-influenced primitivism, Neo-Classicism, jazz, atonality, bitonality and even Serialism. Whatever he did, he excelled at it. He exerted the greatest influence in the musical world, however, as a Neo-Classicist. While the brilliant, coloristic ballets, Firebird (1910), Petrushka (1911), and Le sacre du printemps (1913) (The Rite of Spring, a.k.a. "Pictures of a Pagan Russia") established him as an innovative composer to be reckoned with, it was the *Octet for Wind Instruments* (1922-23) up through *The Rake's Progress* (1951) which earned him the designation of Neo-Classicist.

Igor Stravinsky's Greatest Hits:

> *Pulcinella* (1920)
>
> *Octet for Wind Instruments* (1922-23)
>
> *L'histoire du soldat* (1918)
>
> *Symphony of Psalms* (1930)
>
> Opera:
>> *The Rake's Progress* (1951)
>
> Cantata:
>> *Les noces* (1923)

Stravinsky's Greatest Hits BEFORE *1920: (a.k.a. Expressionist, Primitivist)*

> *The Firebird* (1910)
>
> *Petrushka* (1911)
>
> *Rite of Spring* (1913)

AVANT-GARDE -ISM

This is yet another general term. *Avant-Garde -ISM refers to composers who radically broke with established methods of composition, by using recordings, electronics, chance operations such as rolling the dice to determine notes, and complete serialism á la Schoenberg and Boulez.* Names which pop up are Charles Ives, Edgard Varèse, Henry Cowell, and Milton Babbitt. The Frenchman, Edgard Varèse (1883-1965), pioneered electronic music. He also took the unique view that music was moving bodies of sound as color, mass and its relationship to space. In his *Poème électronique* (1958), the composer placed 425 tape-playing loudspeakers at points in the Philips Pavilion – which had been designed by Le Corbusier – at the Brussels Worlds Fair. The spatial design of the piece reflected the architecture of the building.

The American composer, Henry Cowell (1897-1965), brought new meaning to *tone clusters*: the striking of piano keys with the forearm or the fist. (Is it any wonder that Cage was his pupil?) But he was a Neo-Classicist too! Cowell wrote twenty symphonies, chamber and choral music. Go figure.

ANTI-RATIONALISM

John Cage. So...OUT there! While other composers agonized over notes, Cage punched holes in a star chart over music paper. *Voilà* – a composition! Or how about rolling the dice to make those decisions for you? He did that too. He wrote a piano piece in which not a key is caressed. He fooled around with the guts of the piano, inserting alien, non-musical objects between the strings, giving the instrument a strange, exotic voice. He consulted the *I Ching*, a 700-year old Chinese book of changes and divination, and a general source of wisdom. His great achievement? Where Shakespeare pointed out that all the world's a stage, John Cage showed us that all the world's a piece of music.

Greatest Hits:

> *Amores*
> *4' 33"*
> *HPSCHD*
> *Imaginary Landscape* (for 12 radios)
> *Piano Concert*

NEO-ROMANTICISM

Aside from atonality and serialism lay Neo-Romanticism. Composers turned to their native tongues and music for inspiration and infused these into long-lined, luscious, broad-sweeping, evocative pieces. Rhythms of speech and modal scales often found in folk music were integrated into their music, making it uniquely of their own country and peoples. It happened here in America too, particularly with George Gershwin (1898-1937) and Leonard Bernstein (1918-1990). They integrated jazz idioms into their Classically-grounded music.

Aaron Copland

While Aaron Copland also injected jazz into his earlier works, he eventually turned to another side of America – the heartland: the physical, geographic grandeur and its country folk. The most notable example of this is *Appalachian Spring* (1944), in which he quoted a Shaker hymn melody, "Tis a Gift to Be Simple". Known as his Americana period, it all began with the ballets, *Billy the Kid* (1940) and *Rodeo* (1942), in which the composer used cowboy songs. This period continued with his *Lincoln Portrait* (also 1942) for narrator and orchestra (William F. Buckley enjoys performing the role of narrator), and *Fanfare for the Common Man.*

Beginning in 1937, Copland composed film scores. All the while this great composer, teacher, pianist, speaker and author experimented with serialism, but throughout his career he continually maintained his uniquely American voice.

Greatest Hits:

> *Lincoln Portrait* for orchestra and
> narrator (1942)

Ballets*:*
> *Billy the Kid* (1942)
> *Rodeo* (1942)
> *Appalachian Spring* (1945)
> *Third Symphony* (1946)
>> which incorporates *Fanfare for the*
>> *Common Man* (1942)

Opera:
> *The Second Hurricane* (1937) is an opera
> for high school students

Film Music:

Of Mice and Men (1937)

Our Town (1940)

The Heiress (1949)

Samuel Barber (1910-1981) reflected American industry and jazz in works such as *Excursions* for the piano. Barber's other works of note include: *The School for Scandal* (1933), *Adagio* (1936), two *Symphonies* (1936, 1944), *Concerto for Violin* (1940), *Concerto for Cello* (1945), *Concerto for Piano* (1962), the ballet, *Medea* (1946) written for Martha Graham, and an opera called *Vanessa* (1958) for which Gian Carlo Menotti wrote the libretto.

In Eastern Europe, Béla Bartók (1881-1945) stands by himself. He collected and analyzed Hungarian and other folk music becoming the first ethno-musicologist. Bartók rarely incorporated these folk tunes, but rather they inspired his musical language with their asymmetrical rhythms and chromaticisms. *Concerto for Orchestra, Concerto for Violin and Orchestra* (No. 2), the six String Quartets and *Music for Strings, Percussion and Celesta* (1937) are his most frequently programmed works.

Russia's Romantic tradition was furthered by composer/ pianist Sergei Rachmaninoff (1873-1943) who specialized in brooding and melancholy. His famous *Prelude* in C# minor is the *leitmotiv* for a sinister character named "Carlo Hesser" on ABC's daytime soap, *One Life to Live*.

In the northern climes of Scandinavia, Jean Sibelius (1865-1957) infused his symphonic poems with characteristics of Finland. When you see or hear an ad for Finlandia Swiss Cheese, it is Sibelius' symphonic tone poem, *"Finlandia"*, authenticating it in the background. The consensus is that after 1925 Sibelius composed nothing of significance. His best works are his symphonies, and particularly the Violin Concerto (1903).

Across the North Sea in England were Gustav Holst (of *The Planets* fame) and Ralph Vaughan Williams (1872-1958) (the latter's first name being pronounced like "raif") who all turned to native musical idioms. Vaughan Williams blended traditional English folksongs and hymns with the European traditions of Bach and Handel, Ravel and Debussy – quite a combo – and re-tooled it all into the big, modern English symphonies he is famous for.

Best loved works are: *London Symphony* (1914), *Pastoral Symphony* (1922) and *Fantasia on a Theme of Thomas Tallis* (1909) – Tallis having been a composer active in the 1500s!

Later, Benjamin Britten continued the English choral tradition, but in a new context, among the most important works being: *A Ceremony of Carols* (1942), *Spring Symphony* (1949); the operas, *Peter Grimes* (1945) and *Turn of the Screw* (1954); *War Requiem* (1962) and *Children's Crusade* (1969).

In Italy it was Ottorino Respighi – his *Pines of Rome* is a lush staple in the concert repertoire – and Giacomo Puccini whose operas are universally acclaimed.

From Spain Manuel de Falla (1876-1946) is considered to be THE most important Spanish composer of the 20th Century. He evokes his country through themes inspired by folksongs of Spain in works such as: *Nights in the Gardens of Spain* for Piano and Orchestra (1908-1915), the *Concerto for Harpsichord and Chamber Ensemble* (1923-1926) and The *Three Cornered Hat* (Ballet).

The Romantic/Spanish guitar music of Joaquin Rodrigo (b. 1902) is so popular you can hear it as you fly a major airline and plug in to the Classical channel of the in-flight musical programming.

TRANSCENDENTALISM

Charles Ives

Charles Ives is the musical counterpart of Thoreau, Emerson, Whitman – the New England Transcendentalists of American literature. He was uninfluenced by European music and was ahead of his time, anticipating the likes of Cage in his use of *aleatoric method* (chance). A graduate of Yale, he quickly figured out that he would prefer to be a well-fed musician than a starving one; he made a fortune in the insurance business. He composed through the turn of the century, and had such innovative ideas as the use of *polytonality* (different keys within the same piece), a bit of serialism, unregulated rhythms and quarter tones. Mostly, however, you get the feeling that more than one thing is going on at the same time in his music, such as in *Three Places in New England*, where we hear two bands at once.

Greatest Hits:

> *Three Places in New England*
> *Concord Sonata*
> Four Symphonies
> *The Unanswered Question*
> *Central Park in the Dark*

More -ISM Makers (a.k.a. Generation XX)

Here are some quick sound bites about other composers experimenting in the great aesthetic lab of music:

Frederick Delius(1862-1934)

English. Impressionistic. Came to America to grow oranges. Timber! Oops, that is: *Timbre*! Lyric and sustained moods. Very listenable.

Claim to fame:

> *A Village Romeo and Juliet* (Opera)
> *Concerto for Violin* (1916).

Paul Dukas (1865-1935)

French. Neo-Romantic. Vivid, colorful.

Claim to fame:

The Sorcerer's Apprentice (1897) which accompanied enchanted brooms getting Mickey Mouse in a lot of hot water in a 1953 Disney classic cartoon of the same name.

Gabriel Fauré (1845-1924)

French. Style described as "poetic and evanescent". Reined-in, refined and mostly tonal. A pre-Impressionist, transitional figure who set the stage for Debussy and the 20th Century.

Claim to Fame:

> *Ballade for Piano and Orchestra* (1881)
> *Pelléas et Mélisande* , (Opera - 1887)
> *Requiem Mass* (1887).

Howard Hanson (1898-1981)

Put the Eastman School of Music in Rochester, New York on the map. Wrote in the Romantic tradition.

Claim to Fame:

> *Nordic Symphony* (1922)
> *Romantic Symphony* (1930)
> *Merry Mount* (Opera - 1933)
> *Symphony* No. 4 (1934).

Roy Harris (1898-1980)

The great American symphonist, at least in the 1930s and 1940s.
Captured the American character.

Claim to Fame:

> *Third Symphony* (1938).

Zoltán Kodály (1882-1967)

In Steven Spielberg's *Close Encounters of the Third Kind* (1985), it is the Hungarian Kodály's music education system that enables Us to communicate with Them – making music a truly "universal" language. Worked closely with Bartók, collecting and cataloguing folksongs.

Claim to Fame:

Hary Janos (Comic Opera - 1926)

Gian Carlo Menotti (1911-)

Italian-American opera composer. Controversial founder of the Festival of Two Worlds in Spoleto, Italy and its American counterpart of the same name in Charleston, South Carolina. (He is no longer associated with the latter.) Has a Christmas season gone by without his perennial classic, *Amahl and the Night Visitors* (1951) – the first opera ever composed for T.V.? Writes his own librettos (and others).

Claim to Fame:

The Consul (1950)
The Medium (1946)
The Telephone (1947)
The Saint of Bleecker Street (1954).

Carl Orff (1895-1982)

German known for pulsating, vigorous rhythms, most notably in his tour de force *Carmina Burana* (1937), an oratorio based on very racy 13th Century secular poetry "discovered" in a monastery.

Krzysztof Penderecki (1933)

Polish expressionist. Exploits unusual instrumental sounds for effect.

His *Threnody for the Victims of Hiroshima* (1961) for fifty-two strings is positively eerie.

William Schuman (1910-1992)

American. Won the first Pulitzer Prize for music composition in 1943. Reorganized the Julliard School. Known for symphonic output.

Roger Sessions (1896-1985)

American composer and teacher. Considered to be one of the ultimate American expressionists.

Claim to Fame:

> *Concerto for Orchestra* (1981)
> *Divertimento for Orchestra* (1959-60).

Virgil Thomson (1896-1989)

American. Mr. Neo-Class! Style described as "whimsical, irreverent".

Claim to Fame:

> *Louisiana Story* (1948)
> > Won the only Pulitzer Prize for a film score
> > in 1949 for the documentary,
> *Four Saints in Three Acts* (1934)
> > an opera with libretto by Gertrude Stein.

Heitor Villa-Lobos (1887-1959)

Mostly self-taught Brazilian composer who revolutionized music education in the Brazilian public schools. The Bartók of Brazil in that he collected and documented Native American music and folk music.

Claim to Fame:

> *Bachianas brasileiras* (1930-1945), a blending of
> Bach and powerful rhythms of northeastern
> Brazilian folk music.

Yannis Xenakis (1922-)

Greek known for use of math and computers in his compositions. Studied engineering. Philosophy: *stochastic music*, the goal being *stochos* or evolution to a stable state. Still going strong.

UBTHECMPSR**

No, it is not a typo. It is typical of the way some avant-garde composers name their pieces, computer centers, probably even their pets. Perhaps it stemmed from real estate ads in the Sunday *New York Times:* "4 BDRM APT W/VU." In this case, the translation is "You Be The Composer!" Each piece in this collection of *UBTHECMPSR* comes with composing instructions. Those are just guidelines. The creating is up to you. If you do not follow them exactly, that makes you especially avant-garde.

So, why not try your hand at being yet another innovator of the "Century *sans* identity"? If you time it right, you might become the first "transmillennial" composer! Who knows – you may even make it into future music history books!

Dart Ditty

You will create it in the style of John Cage. Take a piece of manuscript paper or draw a staff onto plain paper, hang it up on a wall or preferably a dart-board, hurl darts at it. Voilà – those are your notes! Color the holes and you have a piece.

To kill two birds with one stone, as it were, hang the New York Stock Exchange or NASDAQ listings behind the manuscript paper, then buy those stocks accordingly. A lot of stockbrokers are composers and vice versa!

Star Search

This piece is another homage to John Cage. Take a star chart (the *New York Times,* for example, usually has a partial one) and lay it over manuscript paper. Get a compass point, knitting needle or anything pointed and sharp; gently punch out any star/constellation you like. Go back over the punched holes with a sharp pencil or pen.

To get your note values, take a single dice and roll it for each note. Whatever comes up is its duration. For example, if you roll two, the note gets two counts. Write it in under each note. You are done.

Everything But The Kitchen Sink

As you might have guessed, this is a piece for prepared piano. It is a type of a recipe for music. If you can get to a grand piano (it will not hurt it), all the better. If not, you can be more creative in getting the materials positioned between the strings so they do not slide down to oblivion. Here are the ingredients you will need:

5 Screws with heads large enough so they do not
    slip through the strings
4 bolts
2 nuts, slipped over two screws
    1 gum eraser sliced in thirds
3 wooden clothespins
3 large rubber bands (to tie around upright piano
    strings)
3 sheets of 8 1/2 x 11 paper or wax paper folded,
    until quite small
Kitchen sponge
Anything else you wish as long as it does not hurt
    the instrument.

Now, place these ingredients between any strings you want to. Scatter them around equally, or bunch them together. Try different combinations. You can hold down the pedals or leave them alone. Play "Mary Had a Little Lamb" or a Bach *Fugue* if you can. Play "Chopsticks" or "Heart and Soul". If you press numerous keys adjacent to one another, resulting in a tone cluster, you will also be honoring composer, Henry Cowell. Do anything you want, it is YOUR musical concoction. So serve it up!

The IVES of March

This piece is especially fun in the fall during football season. You can combine exercise with the creative process. *The IVES of March* pays tribute to that Connecticut Yankee,

Charles Ives, who was especially fond of multi-music experiences, grounded in snippets of the familiar.

Here's the list of necessary gear:

SONY Walkman or similar headphone w/radio

Running or Walking shoes

Timing: This will involve a little initiative on your part - find out when the local high school or college marching band practices outdoors. In my town, it is late afternoon when they march on the football field around which runs the track. Be sure to stretch out, set your radio and go.

The Piece: As you approach the band (the worse the better), marvel at how the radio and band mix and/or fight with each other. Add in your breathing and footfalls and you are really on the multi-sonic track. As you make the turn away from them, notice the conflict or harmony waning. You can vary the experience further by accelerating or decelerating your pace. And if you can "perform" the piece somewhere in New England, all the better.

Coda

What Lies Ahead?

Coda

Epilogue: What Lies Ahead?

Without a doubt, more -ISMs will evolve from this neo-primordial, compositional soup. Unprecedented experimentation in music and music-generators will keep musicologists as busy as Madison Avenue creatives in trying to latch on to the "Big Concept" and its "Buzzword". In the scholarly world of music, no two textbooks approach the period the same way, no two teachers present identical views. It is a compositional deck of cards constantly being shuffled and dealt.

The 20th Century (and probably into the 21st Century) appears to be paralleling the Medieval period in which composers were groping around for a new musical vocabulary and system – trying and rejecting, trying and triumphing. Four hundred years later, it paid off with Haydn, Mozart and then Beethoven.

But what of the 21st Century? Will live concerts as we know them – seated orchestra on a stage – become obsolete because children are audio-visually oriented and cannot tolerate the visually static experience of the concert hall? After all, their grandparents who now occupy the plush seats at the Philharmonic were raised sitting around the radio and using their imaginations. Should programmers then find a way to make Classical music concerts more visually stimulating for television and computer generations?

By going to concerts, listening to Classical radio and compact discs, we are witnessing a collective creative process: getting a peek at musical evolution. No other culture has had such immediate feedback, such direct contact, such *access* to what composers are doing. Things are happening fast. We hear a new piece, we react, the press reacts, the scholars react. Be a part of it. Take the children to concerts. Find the music.

HELP SHAPE THE FUTURE OF MUSIC!

Perform!

    Compose!

        Enjoy! – and

KNOW WHEN TO CLAP!

Help Me, Rondo!

(The Glossary)

"A virtuoso is someone with real high morals."

Elementary school student

Help Me, Rondo!

(The Glossary)

Musical terminology can be SO confusing! Some words not only sound like non-musical words, but LOOK like them as well. So here is a glossary of the most important words you will need, with the particularly confusing ones highlighted:

Absolute music

Music without a story or non-musical connotations.

Adagio

Term used to describe a slow movement.

Aleatory

Also known as CHANCE music. Derived from Latin, *alea* meaning dice. Let your cat walk on your piano, write it down, tah-dah! It is aleatoric!

Allegro

Term used to describe a rapid, brisk movement.

Alto

A lower female voice, also known as contralto. Also refers to instruments of comparable range, i.e. alto saxophone.

Aria

A composition for solo voice, usually with accompaniment.

Atonality

A type of modern music in which traditional tonality is absent.

Avant-garde

Term used to describe the most radical of 20th Century composers.

Baritone

Male voice between bass and tenor.

BASS – Not a game fish

In music (pronounced BASE) there are several meanings: 1. The lowest of the stringed instruments; 2. The lowest of the male voices; 3. The lowest note in a chord.

Cadence

A progression of notes in a piece that gives the effect of conclusion.

CADENZA - Not a coveted piece of office furniture

A flashy, sometimes improvised passage played by the soloist in a concerto.

CANON - Not a big gun

A tightly-controlled form of musical imitation, done in succession at fixed intervals.

Cantata

A vocal work in several movements with instrumental accompaniment, developed in the Baroque. Its content can be sacred or secular.

Cantus firmus

Latin term referring to a fixed melody.

Chamber music

Music intended for performance in a small hall or intimate venue.

Chord

Three or more notes sounding simultaneously.

Chorus

1. A large group singing choral music; 2. A section in opera or oratorio sung by such a group; 3. A refrain in a song, i.e. "Jingle Bells," in which "Dashing through the snow" is the verse, "Oh, jingle bells, jingle bells," is the chorus.

Chromatic

Music involving half-steps, the closest interval between two notes.

Clavier

An early term for a keyboard instrument.

Coda

A concluding section of a movement.

Concertmaster

As you face the stage, the first violinist seated immediately to the left of the conductor.

Concerto

A piece for a solo instrument accompanied by orchestra and usually in three movements.

Concerto grosso

A concerto for a small ensemble of instruments accompanied by orchestra.

Counterpoint

Two or more simultaneous melodies.

Crescendo

Getting louder.

Diminuendo

Literally diminishing. An indication meaning to become quieter.

Dynamics

Levels of volume in music.

Electronic music

Any music that is plugged in.

Étude

Literally, "study," referring to a piece in which a specific challenge is offered to the musician.

Fantasia

A free-formed composition.

Form

The structure of a piece of music; i.e. sonata form, rondo form, *da capo* form.

FUGUE - Not a foreign obscenity

A piece in which the main theme must be imitated and highlighted in each part.

GROUND BASS - Not a fish paté

A pattern of bass notes repeated over and over again.

Harmony

The "vertical" aspect of music, as opposed to the horizontal or melodic aspect. The simultaneous sounding of pitches.

Harpsichord

An early keyboard instrument, in which the strings are plucked, rather than struck as in a piano.

Impromptu

A short piano piece that sounds improvised.

Improvisation

Winging it without notation.

Interval

The variation in pitch between two notes.

INVERSION - Not a weather phenomenon

When the melody is turned upside down, forming a mirror image.

Instrumentation

The combination of instruments used in a piece.

Jazz

20th century American style music created by black Americans combining elements from European, American and tribal African musics. It is often improvised and may have complicated rhythmic structures.

Key

The tonal center of a set pattern of notes (a.k.a. scale), in "major" or "minor".

Largo

A very slow, stately, and broad movement.

Leitmotiv

A musical tag-line.

Libretto

The story or "book" of an opera.

LIED - Not the act of having fibbed

An art-song. (Pronounced LEED).

Madrigal

In the 1600s, a secular piece for small choir.

Major

In Western music's traditional harmony, it is the "happy" sounding key, as opposed to minor, the "sad" sounding key.

Mass

In music, the setting of the Roman Catholic service.

Mazurka

A fast Polish dance in 3/4 time.

Melody

The tune.

Meter

The basic pattern of rhythm in a piece; i. e. three beats to a measure or any number of beats desired by the composer.

Metronome

A device used to indicate the speed of a piece of music.

Mezzo-soprano

A female voice with a range between soprano and alto.

Minuet

An early French dance in 3/4 time.

Modal

A kind of harmony or scale derived neither from major or minor keys.

Modulation

The process of moving from one key to another.

Motet

A sacred, contrapuntal piece sung without accompaniment.

Movement

A section of a composition.

OPUS - Not a really prolific composer

It refers to the categorization of a composer's works, with a number after. Example: Op. 10.

Oratorio

A large, religious choral work with all the artillery: lots of voices, orchestra and soloists.

Ostinato

An incessant (obstinate) repeated pattern of notes around which other notes occur.

Pitch

The high or low quality of a sound.

Polonaise

A stately dance of Polish origin in 3/4 time.

POLYPHONY - Not a multiple imposter

A composition in which two equally important melodies are played simultaneously.

Prelude

A short piece which serves as an introduction. In the 19th century it became its own independent form.

PRESTO - Not a term for pulling a rabbit out of your hat

Term indicating a very fast tempo (speed) of a piece.

Program music

Music that tells a story.

Program notes

In your program, the description and explanation of the music to be performed.

Quarter tone

Half the distance between two consecutive (half-step) keys on the piano.

Recitative

Speech-like singing found in operas, oratorios, cantatas.

Requiem

A composition written for the funeral Mass of the Roman Catholic Church.

Retrograde

A melody presented backwards.

Rhapsody

An instrumental piece in free form, often based on folk songs or native musics.

Rhythm

The pattern of movement in music.

RONDO - Not the girl helping the Beach Boys

A musical form in which a theme is presented several times, with contrasting sections in between.

Rubato

Meaning to "rob". A style of playing characterized by slowing down then speeding up for expressive purposes.

Scale

The series of pitches arranged according to a set pattern.

SCHERZO - Not a person with multiple personalities, i.e. Sybil

A lively movement in 3/4 time.

SCORE – Not the number of goals, hits, strokes, etc.

The written entity of the music.

Secular music

Non-religious in content.

Serialism

In the 20th century, an arrangement of all 12 tones of the chromatic scale. The concept can also be applied to rhythm, duration, density, etc.

Solo

One player or singer.

Sonata

A multi-movement piece in which the first movement consists of an exposition, development, and recapitulation. It can be for piano or other instruments. Symphonies usually employ this form in their first movements.

Song cycle

A collection of art-songs based on a unifying theme.

Soprano

The highest of the female vocal ranges.

SUITE – Not a living room/bedroom/bath combination in a hotel

An instrumental piece with several movements.

Symphonic poem

A one-movement symphonic work which tells a story.

Symphony

A large composition for orchestra.

Synthesizer

An electronic device which can both generate and alter sound.

Tempo

The speed of the beats in music; i.e. how fast the piece moves.

Tenor

The highest male vocal range.

Theme

The main melody.

Toccata

An intense, rapid-fire keyboard piece. Bach's are among the best.

Tone poem

Same as symphonic poem.

TONIC – Not a cure-all for what ails you or your hair – or your gin

The musical focal point around which the whole piece is centered.

TRANSCRIPTION – Not an ancient rite of passage which turns boys into men

Music adapted for an instrument other than that for which it was written.

Tritone

The nails-on-a-blackboard interval of six half-steps between two notes; also known as the devil in music.

Variation

Different treatment of a given theme.

VIBRATO - Not a sex toy

A tremulous effect in singing or on stringed instruments for expression.

VIRGINAL - Not a pristine maiden

An early harpsichord.

VIRTUOSO - Not someone with exemplary moral behavior

A big-time technician in voice or on an instrument. If it is a female, call her a virtuos**a**. If there is more than one, call them virtuos**i**.

Bibliography

Apel, Willi, ed., *Harvard Dictionary of Music*, Cambridge: The Belknap Press of Harvard University Press, 1979.

Brown, Howard M., *Music in the Renaissance*, Saddle River: Prentice-Hall, Inc., 1976.

Croften, Ian, ed. and Fraser, Donald, ed., *A Dictionary of Musical Quotations*, New York: Schirmer Books, 1989.

Einstein, Alfred, *Music in the Romantic Era*, New York: W. W. Norton & Company, Inc., 1947.

Greene, David Mason, *Greene's Biographical Encyclopedia of Composers,* New York: Doubleday & Company, Inc., 1985.

Grout, Donald Jay, *A Short History of Opera*, New York: Columbia University Press, 1965.

Grout, Donald Jay and Palisca, Claude V., *A History of Western Music*, New York: W. W. Norton & Company, Inc., 1988.

Holoman, D. Kern, *Evenings With the Orchestra*, New York: W. W. Norton & Company, Inc., 1992.

Hoppin. Richard H., *Medieval Music*, New York: W. W. Norton & Company, Inc., 1978.

Hoppin, Richard H., ed., *Anthology of Medieval Music*, New York: W. W. Norton & Company, Inc., 1978.

Longyear, Rey Morgan, *Nineteenth-Century Romanticism in Music*, Saddle River: Prentice-Hall, Inc., 1973.

Parrish, Carl, ed. and Ohl, John F., ed., *Masterpieces of Music Before 1750*, New York: W. W. Norton & Company, Inc., 1951.

Sadie, Stanley, ed., *The New Grove Dictionary of Music*, London: Macmillan Publishers, Ltd., 1980.

Sadie, Stanley, ed., *The Norton / Grove Concise Encyclopedia of Music*, London: Macmillan Press, Ltd., 1991.

Salzman, Eric, *Twentieth-Century Music*, Saddle River: Prentice-Hall, Inc., 1974.

Simon, Henry W., ed., The Victor Book of The Opera. New York: Simon & Schuster, Inc., 1976.

Slonimsky, Nicolas. Lectionary of Music. New York: McGraw-Hill Publishing Company, 1989.

Zorn, Jay D. The Music Listener's Companion. Saddle River: Prentice-Hall, Inc., 1988.

Index

Manilow, Barry 72
Mendelssohn, Felix 26, 81-83, 86
Mendelssohn-Bartholdy, Felix. *See Mendelssohn, Felix*
Menotti, Gian Carlo 131, 140, 144
Messiaen, Olivier 135
Milhaud, Darius 135
Monteverdi, Claudio 38, 44, 74
Mozart, Wolfgang Amadeus 6, 9, 22, 27, 34, 57, 58, 59, 60, 61-63, 64, 66, 67, 73, 74, 80, 108, 125, 126, 153
Mussorgsky, Modest 114

N
Neville, Aaron 73
Nietzsche, Friedrich 98

O
Obrecht, Jacob 36
Ockeghem, Johannes 36, 37, 40
Orff, Carl 144

P
Pachelbel, Johann 46
Paganini, Niccolò 73, 87
Palestrina, Giovanni Pierluigi da 36, 37, 40
Pavarotti, Luciano 3
Penderecki, Krzysztof 144
Peri, Jacopo 44
Perle, George 126
Petrucci, Ottaviano de 38
Porter, Cole 130
Poulenc, Francis 135
Prez, Josquin des 36, 37, 40
Prokofiev, Sergei 124, 125, 136

Puccini, Giacomo 72, 74, 102-104
Purcell, Henry 45, 53, 112

R
Rachmaninoff, Sergei 16, 140
Rameau, Jean-Philippe 46
Ravel, Maurice 114, 134, 141
Reich, Steve 133
Respighi, Ottorino 141
Riley, Terry 133
Rimsky-Korsakov, Nikolai 114, 115
Rodrigo, Joaquin 141
Rossini, Gioacchino 74, 86, 97-98

S
Saint-Saëns, Camille 112, 113
Salieri, Antonio 68, 78
Sammartini, Giovanni Battista 68
Sand, George 89
Satie, Erik 134
Scarlatti, Alessandro 46
Scarlatti, Domenico 46
Schickele, Peter 6
Schoenberg, Arnold 71, 126, 128, 131, 132, 133, 135
Schubert, Franz 3, 68, 74, 78-80, 92, 108
Schuman, William 145
Schumann, Clara Wieck 84, 85, 89, 93
Schumann, Robert 72, 75, 77, 80, 84-85, 86, 88, 92, 93, 98, 108
Schutz, Heinrich 45
Serkin, Rudolph 75
Sessions, Roger 145
Shakespeare, William 82, 83, 86
Shostakovich, Dmitri 136
Sibelius, Jean 133, 140